Practice Test #1

Practice Questions

Reading Test

Questions 1-3pertain to the following passage:

During difficult economic times, a company may apply to the court for Chapter 11 bankruptcy. This legal filing, a part of the United States bankruptcy law, protects the firm from all creditors while it attempts to reorganize its business and then repay its debts.

By filing Chapter 11, a company will not be closed down due to the outstanding funds it owes to a creditor. While the firm is under the protection of Chapter 11, it will usually make sweeping changes throughout the company. Employees may be laid off or fired, management may be consolidated, buildings may be sold off, and employee benefits may be affected. All changes within the company are designed to return it to profitability, repay creditors, and continue to remain viable.

1. What is the main idea of the passage?
    a. An overview of Chapter 11
    b. Why a company will file for Chapter 11
    c. Legal rules associated with filing Chapter 11
    d. What happens after a Chapter 11 filing
    e. Creditors' rights with Chapter 11

2.When a company is in Chapter 11, executives will make changes mainly:
    a. To work toward solvency
    b. To save money
    c. To ensure their salaries remain intact
    d. To keep creditors at bay
    e. To create a smaller company

3.Which statement about the passage is not true?
    a. Creditors do not get paid during Chapter 11 proceedings
    b. Chapter 11 is a legal filing
    c. After a business reorganizes, most debts will be repaid
    d. Management is often changed during reorganization
    e. Employee benefits are usually unaffected during Chapter 11

Copyright © Mometrix Media. You have been licensed one copy of this document for personal use only. Any other reproduction or redistribution is strictly prohibited. All rights reserved.

Questions 4-5 pertain to the following passage:

To "take the Fifth" means to refuse to testify against oneself in court. A person cannot be forced to testify in court if that testimony will be self-incriminating. The Fifth Amendment of theConstitution states this basic principle of United States law.

The Miranda decision, a 1966 Supreme Court ruling, states that under the Fifth Amendment, a suspect in police custody has the right to remain silent and to consult an attorney and that anything the person says can be used against him or her in court. This information is recited to suspects before police officers ask them any questions.

Aside from protecting a person in custody and in a court of law, prohibiting self-incrimination ensures that the prosecution is responsible for the burden of proof.

4.According to the passage, which of the following is true?
    a. People cannot be forced to testify in court
    b. Suspects in police custody must answer police questions
    c. The Miranda decision and "take the fifth" are the same thing
    d. The Fifth Amendment was added in 1966
    e. The Miranda decision protects suspects in police custody

5.What is the main purpose of this passage?
    a. To explain self-incrimination
    b. To discuss our legal system
    c. To explain how the Miranda decision came from the Fifth Amendment
    d. To provide details of the 1966 Supreme Court case
    e. To discuss suspects' rights

Question 6 pertains to the following passage:

A topographic map is designed to showcase the surface features of a specific land area. These types of maps feature the area's geography and highlight political boundaries, roads, highways, railroads, bodies of water, and some buildings. The maps show the relative positions and elevations of the natural and manmade features of the area.

6. Which of the following would be the best introductory sentence for this passage?
    a. Many maps include typographic details
    b. Use a topographic map if you plan to hike in a new area
    c. Comparing two areas is easy with a topographic map
    d. Topographic maps are usually the most inclusive of all map types
    e. Most topographic maps are made usingcomputers

Copyright © Mometrix Media. You have been licensed one copy of this document for personal use only. Any other reproduction or redistribution is strictly prohibited. All rights reserved.

Question 7 pertains to the following passage:

The classic opera *Madame Butterfly* was written by Giacomo Puccini. In the opus, an American naval officer stationed in Japan falls in love with Butterfly, a Japanese woman. He returns to America but promises to come back to marry her. When the soldier does return to Japan three years later, he is accompanied by his American wife. Shocked and humiliated, Butterfly stabs herself. She dies in the soldier'sarms as he begs her to forgive him.

7. This passage describes characters' feelings in *Madame Butterfly* as all of the following
   EXCEPT:
   a. Romantic
   b. Poignant
   c. Crushing
   d. Musical
   e. Tragic

Questions 8-9 pertain to the following passage:

De facto segregation, which literally means segregation "by fact," occurs when a specific socioeconomic group resides in an area with other families of that same demographic. Students living in those areas will typically end up going to neighborhood schools comprised of children of one minority group or one income level. Because it was not considered direct discrimination, de facto segregation was not considered unconstitutional.

De facto segregation was a particularly serious problem in the racially-charged 1960s. Many elementary schools were completely racially segregated, especially in the South, with African Americans attending all-black schools, while white students attended all-white schools.Most people agreed that these schools had vast differences in buildings, materials, and staff, with students from higher-income neighborhoods enjoying an education in what can be described as a higher quality setting than their less-affluent peers at other schools. Although not often discussed, de facto segregation can still be found in our country.

8.According to the passage, which of the following is an example of de facto segregation?
   a. Large schools
   b. Separate schools
   c. Diverse schools
   d. Integrated schools
   e. Heterogeneous schools

Copyright © Mometrix Media. You have been licensed one copy of this document for personal use only. Any other reproduction or redistribution is strictly prohibited. All rights reserved.

9.According to the passage, which of the following is true?
   a. De facto segregation happens today
   b. De facto segregation was never a serious problem
   c. De facto segregation was a problem only for high income students
   d. De facto segregation is always characterized by race
   e. De facto segregation creates equality

Question 10 pertains to the following passage:

Corrosion is the deterioration of a metal. This decay can be easily seen on pots, pans, jewelry, and silverware. Iron corrodes when it comes into contact with water and oxygen, with the decomposition present as rust. Copper corrodes when it is exposed to the elements, and the decay is present as a green sheen. Silver tarnishes, or corrodes after a period of time, with its deterioration apparent in a dull black covering of the silver surface.

10. Which of the following is not stated as a reason for corrosion?
   a. Exposure to elements
   b. Passage of time
   c. Deterioration from heat
   d. Contact with water
   e. Contact with air

Question 11 pertains to the following passage:

A market economy, also called a "free economy," is one in which individuals and corporations control the production, marketing, and distribution of goods and services within a society. There is a minimum of government interference in a market economy. Competition between markets keeps prices at a particular level. When prices become too high, consumers will not purchase goods, which forces sellers to adjust prices to a level where consumers will buy.

Market economies have minimal government involvement; this type of economic system still requires some federal regulation. A complete market economy would mean there would be no government regulation or taxation, two components necessary to ensure that the economy keeps running.

Copyright © Mometrix Media. You have been licensed one copy of this document for personal use only. Any other reproduction or redistribution is strictly prohibited. All rights reserved.

11. Which is a true statement about a market economy?
    a. Sellers determine price
    b. Government determines price
    c. Corporations determine price
    d. Individuals determine price
    e. Competition determines price

Questions 12-13 pertain to the following passage:

In literature, the problem, usually referred to as the conflict, should be introduced in the early paragraphs of a story and should directly involve the main character. Throughout the story, the main character should seek to determine how the conflict will be resolved. The conflict resolution should not be obvious to the reader; instead, the reader should wonder how things are going to work out and should be connected enough with the main character so that the character's actions matter.

By the end of the story, the main character should have somehow grown or changed, even just a little, from the experience. Stories in which the main character repeats the lesson he or she has learned often do not work as well as stories in which growth or change is inferred. Most readers enjoy thinking about the way a conflict has been resolved and come to their own conclusions after mulling it over for a period of time. When the resolution is simply stated at the end of astory, the reader often ends up with little or nothing to think about.

12. What is the best way to describe conflict?
    a. It is a story situation
    b. It is a story problem
    c. It is a resolution
    d. It is the character's growth process
    e. It is an experience

13. According to the passage, what is one important element of a good story?
    a. A story in which the lesson learned is narrated by the main character
    b. A story with a problem embedded in the middle
    c. A story with a few different conflicts
    d. A story with a predictable resolution
    e. A story in which the main character matters to the reader

Copyright © Mometrix Media. You have been licensed one copy of this document for personal use only. Any other reproduction or redistribution is strictly prohibited. All rights reserved.

Questions 14-17 pertains to the following passage:

Journalists often use a recording device to capture the audio transcript of an interview with a subject. The recording device is thought of as a reliable and efficient way to ensure that all important parts of the interview have been archived which issomething that may be complicated for a journalist to do by hand. Besides being difficult to execute quickly, legibly, and efficiently, taking notes by hand can distract the journalist from the interview subject's body language, verbal cues, or other subtle information that can go unnoticed when the journalist is not fully concentrating on the person talking. These missed cuesfor example, noticing that the tough-guy interview subject closed his eyes and trembled slightly, when he talked about his recently departed motherhave added an interesting perspective to the article about him.

Relying on a recording device is not without troubles; however, most journalists can quickly relate stories of disappointments they or co-workers have endured due to problems with equipment. For instance, a journalist may not notice low batteries until it is too late. As a result, a portion of an interview can be lost without any way to reclaim it. The machine's volume can be accidentally left too low to hear the subject on later playback, the recorder may be accidentally switched off during the interview, and any number of other unplanned and unexpected electronic malfunctions can occur to sabotage the recording. While recording device problems may not occur often, even a rate of once a year can be extremely problematic for a writer. Some glitches may be unrealized until hours later when the journalist is prepared to work with the recording.

Most experienced journalists do not rely solely on technology when they are interviewing a subject for an article. Instead, as the recording device creates an audio record of the interview, journalists will simultaneously record their own notes by hand. This dual-note method means that most of the time, a wise journalist has two good resources to use as he or she writes the article draft.

14.According to the passage, which of the following is not a reason a recording device can be superior to taking notes by hand?
    a. Note taking can be slow
    b. Note taking is unreliable
    c. Note taking forces the writer to look away from the subject
    d. Note taking can cause body language to go unnoticed
    e. Note taking can be difficult to read later

Copyright © Mometrix Media. You have been licensed one copy of this document for personal use only. Any other reproduction or redistribution is strictly prohibited. All rights reserved.

15. Which of the following is not an example of body language?
    a. A quiet answer
    b. Shocked look
    c. Wringing hands
    d. Blinking eyes
    e. A glance to the side

16. What is the best way journalists can ensure that all interview notes will be available to them when they need them?
    a. Taking notes by hand and also recording them
    b. Bringing recorder batteries regularly
    c. Bringing an extra tape for the recorder
    d. Making sure the volume is set on high
    e. Taping the recorder switch to the *On* position

17. Which title is the best choice for this passage?
    a. The Art of Writing Notes
    b. Conducting an Interview
    c. Tape Recording an Interview
    d. Body Language is Important
    e. Problems with Interviews

Questions 18-19 pertain to the following passage:

Florence is not the capital of Italy, but from the fourteenth to the sixteenth centuries, it was the heart of the Italian Renaissance. During those years, the city burgeoned with creativity, and great artists and writers whose works came to be considered classics were active in Florence. Michelangelo, Botticelli, Raphael, da Vinci, and the Medici family called the city their home and were among those responsible for its cultural dominance at the time.

Today, tourists still flock to Florence, which is located in the center of Italy on the Arno River, to view the cathedrals, buildings, and other works of architecture that has been preservedlargely in excellent condition. Artists of all kinds continue to be attracted to Florence as an inspirational place to practice their craft.

18. What is not true about Florence?
    a. It has a rich cultural history
    b. It is an artistic center
    c. It is centrally located
    d. It is the capital of Italy
    e. It is still relevant

Copyright © Mometrix Media. You have been licensed one copy of this document for personal use only. Any other reproduction or redistribution is strictly prohibited. All rights reserved.

19. As it is used in the passage, what does "burgeoned" most nearly mean?
    a. Dwindled
    b. Stagnated
    c. Originated
    d. Deteriorated
    e. Exploded

Question 20 pertains to the following passage:

      Scaffolding is tactical support method used by teachers to assist students so that they are able to successfully accomplish a particular task they would not be able to complete independently. As they scaffold, teachers assess the type and amount of assistance individual students will need to correctly perform a task or respond to a question. The goal is not simplyfor the student to accomplish the single task, but to internalize the skills needed to complete comparable tasks in the future. Scaffolding may entail cues, comments, or other directives designed to guide the student to a particular response.

20. Which of the following sentences would be a relevant detail to add as the second sentence to the paragraph above?
    a. Scaffolding is individual instruction for the weakest students
    b. Students will want to use scaffolding methods in all their learning
    c. Teachers are able to assess students' needs individually when scaffolding
    d. Students appreciate the help
    e. Scaffolding is done quietly and is unnoticed by many students

Question 21 pertains to the following passage:

      The U.S. Department of State is a part of the executive branch of the federal government. Commonly referred to as the State Department, it is headed by the Secretary of State who is appointed by the president. The State Department's chief responsibility is United States foreign policy with some of the duties of the department being to confer with foreign government leaders, maintain a good relationship with America's allies, negotiate treaties, and provide aid to countries in need of help after a disaster, war, or other catastrophic occurrence. Such help may be in the form of economic aid or food.

Copyright © Mometrix Media. You have been licensed one copy of this document for personal use only. Any other reproduction or redistribution is strictly prohibited. All rights reserved.

21. According to the passage, what is the main role of the State Department?
    a. Economic aid
    b. Food
    c. Disaster help
    d. Foreign policy
    e. Treaty negotiation

Questions 22-23 pertain to the following passage:

The concept of gravity intrigued great thinkers even in the earliest of times. Although Aristotle did not accurately determine why objects fall down toward the earth, he did give those researchers who came after him an excellent starting point to move from.

Galileo was especially influenced by the idea of gravity and its relevance to the world. He was able to show not only that the earth is subject to the pull of gravity, but also that other planets are as well. Galileo confirmed that Earth is not a solitary celestial entity, asthere are other large bodies in the solar system that also experienced the same type of gravitational forces. Although parts of his findings were eventually disproven, Galileo's work nevertheless advanced the scientific world's understanding of gravity.

Taking the ideas of Aristotle and Galileo into account, Isaac Newton continued to study the forces, properties, and principles that rule Earth. His First and Second Laws of Motion were the result of many years of study.

22. Based on the information given, what is a celestial entity?
    a. A body in space
    b. A star grouping
    c. A cosmic alien
    d. A solar flare
    e. A star unit

23. Based on the information in the passage, which statement is true?
    a. Galileo's work was proven to be entirely false by later scientists and researchers
    b. Aristotle and Galileo may have known each other
    c. The First and Second Laws of Motion were influenced by Galileo's studies
    d. Galileo's ideas are not relevant in the modern world
    e. The earth is the only large body that experiences gravitational pulls.

Copyright © Mometrix Media. You have been licensed one copy of this document for personal use only. Any other reproduction or redistribution is strictly prohibited. All rights reserved.

Question 24 pertains to the following passage:

Within the next decade, many jobs and careers in the STEM (science, technology, engineering, and math) industries will lack adequately trained workers. Thisproblem has been steadily increasing for years. Most big companies have anticipated that the ways in which the decrease in the number of high school graduates choosing a STEM discipline as their major in college willeventually affect the business world. The government is also taking notice of this declining interest in STEM careers.A federally-commissioned study concluded that both the present STEM workforce is aging, and the number of trained applicants to fill those jobs continues to dwindle.

24. Which magazine listed below would be the best fit for this article?
   a. *Parents* magazine
   b. *Teen* magazine
   c. *Teaching PreK-8*
   d. *High School Guidance Counselor*
   e. *Discovery Science*

Question 25 pertains to the following passage:

Conflicts between students occur every day in most schools across the country. Because the conflicts can vary in severity, some do notnecessarily require someone in authority to intercede. However, some conflicts can be quite and conflict mediation is necessary to arbitrate the problem.

25. Which statement is most likely to appear next in the text?
   a. Some students get hurt in school fights
   b. Conflict mediation can stop all school disputes
   c. Teachers should not have to deal with these problems
   d. Students get themselves into all kinds of scuffles with their peers
   e. Conflict mediation is an effective method of solving school disputes

Copyright © Mometrix Media. You have been licensed one copy of this document for personal use only. Any other reproduction or redistribution is strictly prohibited. All rights reserved.

Today, most everyone with a cell phone has the capability to send and receive text messages. High school students may be the biggest users of this technology. Some parents have had to impose limits on their teen, which oftentimes easily exceeds the three to five hundred text messages allotted to many family plans each month. A flat fee will usually cover this set number of messages, but each additional message may cost twentyor twenty-five cents an amount that can add up to a staggering figure in a short period of time if a user is texting with wild abandon.

These days, most high school teachers do not permit students to bring cell phones into the classroom Students may spend more time texting friends rather than payattention to what is happening in class. Some savvy students have figured out ways to text-message peers inconspicuously and share test answers. Most students would probably agree that there is no reason to have their cell phones with them during the school day; however, most are reluctant leave their phones in their lockers.

Typing a message into a phone was an unheard of communication method even two decades ago. Today, many young users may not remember life without it.

26. To whom is this passage probably being written?
   a. Those who are in favor of cell phone use in schools
   b. Those who are against cell phone use in schools
   c. Those that are in favor of text messaging in school
   d. Those that are against text messaging in school
   e. The passage is not written to any of these audiences

27. What is the best title for this passage?
   a. Texting Problems
   b. Cell Phones Can Spell Trouble
   c. Texting and Students
   d. Teacher Beware
   e. Technology Today

Copyright © Mometrix Media. You have been licensed one copy of this document for personal use only.
Any other reproduction or redistribution is strictly prohibited. All rights reserved.

Questions 28-29 pertain to the following passage:

Many female marathon runners today may not realize that the Boston Marathon was not always open to women participants. It was not until 1972 that women were welcome to register and officially participate in the race. Before that, some women would attempt to take part in the race in ways that would not divulge their gender. One method was registering with just their first initial and last name. In almost all instances, this type of deception was discovered and the runner was disqualified.

28. Based on what is discussed in the passage, which statement is most likely to be true?
   a. Those that used deception to run in the Boston Marathon were arrested
   b. There are women alive today who ran as men in the Boston Marathon
   c. No women ran in the Boston Marathon prior to 1972
   d. The Boston Marathon is still biased toward men
   e. Women runners probably never wanted to race in the Boston Marathon

29. According to the passage, what best describes the actions most women took so that they could run in the Boston Marathon prior to 1972?
   a. Lie about their gender
   b. Bribe race officials
   c. Run with a male
   d. Hide from officials
   e. Threaten officials with lawsuits if they are not granted entry into the race

Question 30 pertains to the following passage:

Writing an online journal is a difficult way to make money. Money is certainly not the goal of every blogger, but a good blog with a large audience can provide an extra income to those who work at it.

If a blogger is able to prove that he or she consistently has a large number of readers who check the blog every few days, the blogger may be able to attract advertisers. These advertisers can be a valuable source of income for the blogger since the online ads will be seen by many people each day.

30. According to the passage, which of the following statements is true?
   a. All blogs make money
   b. Popular blogs can make money for the blogger
   c. All bloggers want to earn an income by blogging
   d. Online advertisements are not income producers
   e. Companies can be easily convinced to advertise on a blog

Copyright © Mometrix Media. You have been licensed one copy of this document for personal use only. Any other reproduction or redistribution is strictly prohibited. All rights reserved.

Questions 31-34 pertain to the following passage:

Swiss psychologist Carl Jung coined the terms "extrovert" and "introvert" to describe characteristics he identified and classified in people's personalities.

Imagine a restaurant buffet table full of a variety of breakfast food selections. One woman walks over to the table and immediately talks with a chef creating omelets to order. After she orders her omelet, the woman turns and talks with another stranger on her left and then to one on her right. She loudly thanks the chef after he slides the omelet onto her plate. Another woman slips into the buffet line and observes those ahead of her as they lift the lids from the food warmers. She moves through the line silently and then takes her seat with her group.

Jung described an extrovert, such as the woman who talked to people she did not know, as one whose actions are external and apparent. He said that in general, extroverts tend to make friends and establish connections with other people with relative ease. Extroverts are able to assess social situations and make an easy adjustment to being with groups of people. Theytypically demonstrate an obvious interest in their surroundings and often act without much forethought.

Introverts tend to be more thoughtful than extroverts, and many of their decisions are processed internal without outwardly apparent signs. Introverts will think of what to do in certain situations before they act. Most introverts are more comfortable keeping to themselves than socializing with other people.

31. Which profession is most likely to be chosen by an introvert?
    a. A stand-up comedian
    b. An event organizer
    c. A Master of Ceremonies
    d. A painter
    e. A street musician

32. According to the passage, which is a true statement?
    a. Introverts rarely have friends
    b. Extroverts are bored without people around
    c. Introverts and extroverts do not get along
    d. Extroverts are insensitive people
    e. Introverts like solitary tasks

Copyright © Mometrix Media. You have been licensed one copy of this document for personal use only. Any other reproduction or redistribution is strictly prohibited. All rights reserved.

33. What do the words "extrovert" and "introvert" describe?
    a. Degrees of personal happiness
    b. Personality characteristics
    c. Demographic classifications
    d. Cultural differences
    e. Perceived intelligence

34. According to the passage, what is true about an extrovert's actions?
    a. They are apparent
    b. They are completely subconscious
    c. They are secretive
    d. They are admired by everyone around them
    e. They are kind and caring

Questions 35-40 pertain to the following passage:

Elementary grade students should be able to describe today's weather, as well as the climate of the area in whichthey live. Depending on their developmental level, students should be able to provide information about whether they live in a dry and hot climate, a tropical climate, or a climate with warm summers and cold winters, often referred to as a continental climate. Students should recognize there are a large number of factors that can affect climate such as: the land and water features of a region, ocean currents, the latitude of an area, and different landforms that may be present.

Students should be aware of how these aspects affect the climate. Elevation is an interesting subject for students to consider. Students should discuss how those areas with a high elevation and close proximity to the equator will experience climatic conditions that are different fromthose areas with a low elevation that arealso located near the equator. Ocean currents can have an effect on a region's climate, and mountain ranges can buffer winds, often causing an area to be warmer than the same area without suchwind shields. Teachers should strive to help students develop a clear understanding about how climate and weather are related but have different meanings.

35. Who is the most likely intended audience for this passage?
    a. Parents
    b. Students
    c. Teachers
    d. School district administrators
    e. University instructors

Copyright © Mometrix Media. You have been licensed one copy of this document for personal use only. Any other reproduction or redistribution is strictly prohibited. All rights reserved.

36. According to the passage above, what is a true statement about students in elementary schools?
    a. All students should be able to talk about the climate of their area and other areas
    b. All students should be able to describe current weather conditions
    c. All students should be able to tell how mountains affect climate
    d. All students should be able to explain how landforms affect climate
    e. All statements are true

37. Which word best describes seasonal climate, like that of the northeast United States?
    a. Tropical
    b. Dry
    c. Hot
    d. Mild
    e. Continental

38. According to the passage, what can mountains do to an area's climate?
    a. Block the wind and make it mild
    b. Blockthe wind and make it warmer
    c. Increase the wind and make it milder
    d. Increase the wind and make it warmer
    e. Nothing

39. Of the choices listed, which one does not have an effect on an area's climate?
    a. Weather balloons
    b. Ocean currents
    c. An area's elevation
    d. Mountain ranges
    e. Proximity to the equator

40. Which word best describes the relationship between the words weather and climate?
    a. They are synonyms
    b. They are antonyms
    c. They are homonyms
    d. They are homophones
    e. They are related word

Copyright © Mometrix Media. You have been licensed one copy of this document for personal use only. Any other reproduction or redistribution is strictly prohibited. All rights reserved.

Writing Test

In the following section, there are underlined parts to each sentence.One of the underlined parts is incorrectly written.Choose the letter that corresponds with the incorrect underlined part of the sentence. If the entire sentence is correct as written, choose E for No error.

41. <u>Nobody</u><u>could have</u> anticipated <u>the extent</u> of the <u>storm's damage</u>. <u>No error</u>
A B   C   D   E

42. <u>Most people</u><u>believed</u> that the game would <u>end up</u> being <u>cancelled</u>. <u>No error</u>
A B   C   D   E

43. We <u>gawked at</u> him as he <u>drug</u> the picnic table <u>closer to</u> the <u>grill area</u>. <u>No error</u>
A B   C   D   E

44. <u>Her bicycle basket</u> was <u>loaded down</u> with books and materials <u>to return</u><u>to</u> the
ABC   D
library. <u>No error</u>
E

45. <u>Her Grandmother</u> ordered <u>monogrammed towels</u> as a gift for the <u>upcoming</u>
ABC
<u>bridal</u>shower. <u>No error</u>
D   E

46. We must <u>ensure that</u> Mike <u>proceeds</u> Ann when the students <u>line up</u> for the
A   B   C
<u>graduation ceremony</u>. <u>No error</u>
D E

47. He was <u>discrete</u> in what he <u>said and wrote</u> since he was <u>not yet sure</u> of his <u>role</u>.
ABCD
<u>No error</u>
E

48. When <u>funding</u> becomes <u>available</u>, we anticipate receiving a new <u>dual-control</u> car
A B C
for our <u>driver training program</u>. <u>No error</u>
D   E

Copyright © Mometrix Media. You have been licensed one copy of this document for personal use only. Any other reproduction or redistribution is strictly prohibited. All rights reserved.

49. Many students <u>yawned, dozed</u>, or talked <u>during</u> the assembly <u>because they were</u>
A BC

<u>disinterested in the speaker's message.</u> <u>No error</u>
D E

50. Since school vacation is <u>eminent, teachers have</u> difficulty <u>getting students to</u> pay
A B

<u>attention to their lessonsduring the last few weeks of school.</u> <u>No error.</u>
CD E

51. Marcy <u>believed</u> her parents <u>had ought</u> to <u>have told her</u> she was still <u>grounded</u> for
A B C   D

the weekend. <u>No error</u>
E

52. <u>Fourteen peoplehangedseven heavy pictures</u> on the <u>interior walls</u> of the lecture
A B C   D

room. <u>No error</u>
E

53. The <u>entire classdisagrees withDr. Olson's views about</u> the <u>future of the mining</u>
A BCD

industry in our area.<u>No error</u>
E

54. I <u>was shockedto realize</u> I <u>had run</u> much <u>further than</u> my two running buddies.
AB   C   D

<u>No error</u>
 E

55. <u>Briana saysless childrenenrolled</u> in our camp program this summer <u>than</u> last
A B   C   D

summer. <u>No error</u>
E

56. The mayor <u>stopped by</u> and gave <u>our principala complimentabout the</u>
 A   B C D

interesting landscaping in front of the school. <u>No error</u>
E

57. <u>Our itineraryshows that</u> we will be at the <u>capitol building</u> all day <u>on Thursday</u>.
A B C D

<u>No error</u>
E

Copyright © Mometrix Media. You have been licensed one copy of this document for personal use only.
Any other reproduction or redistribution is strictly prohibited. All rights reserved.

58. <u>That area</u> with the <u>huge sign</u> will be <u>the sight</u> of our new <u>cultural center</u>.
 A B C D
<u>No error</u>
E

59. The <u>teaching staff</u> included <u>two aidswho helped</u> out in any classroom <u>whenever</u>
A   B C D
they were needed. <u>No error</u>
E

Directions for questions 60 – 78 are as follows:
   The upcoming sentences are given to measure your ability to convey
   the meaning <u>correctly and efficiently</u>.When you choose your answer,
   remember that the sentences should utilize conventional written
   English, including grammar, word selection, sentence structure, and
   punctuation.

   Either a section or a complete sentence <u>will be </u>underlined.Beneath
   the sentences are five answer choices.The first choice (A) will be the
   same as the underlined section. The remaining selectionsprovide
   different substitutions that could replace the underlined section.

   Choose the letter that corresponds with answer that best conveys the
   meaning of the original sentence.If the original wording is the best,
   select answer choice A.If not, select one of the other choices.The
   correct answer is the one that keeps the original meaning and makes
   the sentence the most effective.Make sure your choice makes the
   sentence understandable without being cumbersome or unclear.

60.When he accepted the award, Mr. Stewart <u>said "that he had never been so</u>
   <u>wonderfully honored in hislife</u>."
   a. said "that he had never been so wonderfully honored in my life."
   b. said that "he had never been so wonderfully honored in his life."
   c. said that "he had never been so wonderfully honored in my life."
   d. said that he had "never been so wonderfully honored in my life."
   e. said that he had never been so wonderfully honored in his life.

61.Jake <u>borrowed his parents</u> car without permission so they had no way to get to
work.
   a. borrowed his parents car
   b. borrowed his parent's car
   c. borrowed the parents car
   d. borrowed his Parents car
   e. borrowed his parents' car

Copyright © Mometrix Media. You have been licensed one copy of this document for personal use only.
Any other reproduction or redistribution is strictly prohibited. All rights reserved.

62. <u>Irregardless of the weather</u>, we will still hold the picnic at the park.
   a. Irregardless of the weather,
   b. Irregardless because of the weather,
   c. Irregardless of weather
   d. Regardless of the weather,
   e. Regarding the weather

63. <u>George sounded excited as he tells his mother</u> about the trip to the factory.
   a. George sounded excited as he tells his mother
   b. George sounded excited and he tells his mother
   c. George sounds excited as he told his mother
   d. George sounds excited and he told his mother
   e. George sounded excited as he told his mother

64. <u>Feeling weak after running in the long race.</u>
   a. Feeling weak after running in the long race.
   b. Feeling weak since she had been running in the long race.
   c. Feeling weak on account of running in the long race.
   d. She was feeling weak on account of running in the long race.
   e. She was feeling weak after running in the long race.

65. <u>The leaves were raked all day by Sergio and Gina.</u>
   a. The leaves were raked all day by Sergio and Gina.
   b. The leaves were being raked all day by Sergio and Gina.
   c. Sergio and Gina raked leaves all day.
   d. Sergio and Gina had raked leaves all day.
   e. Leaves were raked all day by Sergio and Gina.

66. <u>Her hand-sewn dress was beautiful she was proud to wear it to the dinner party</u>.
   a. Her hand-sewn dress was beautiful she was proud to wear it to the dinner party.
   b. Her hand-sewn dress was beautiful, she was proud to wear it to the dinner party.
   c. Her hand-sewn dress was beautiful; she was proud to wear it to the dinner party.
   d. Her hand-sewn dress was beautiful so that therefore she was proud to wear it to the dinner party.
   e. Her hand-sewn dress was beautiful but she was proud to wear it to the dinner party.

Copyright © Mometrix Media. You have been licensed one copy of this document for personal use only. Any other reproduction or redistribution is strictly prohibited. All rights reserved.

67. "<u>I hope we find Boots." "He'll be a hungry and tired cat if he spends the night out here,"</u>
   a. "I hope we find Boots." "He'll be a hungry and tired cat if he spends the night out here,"
   b. "I hope we find Boots." He'll be a hungry and tired cat if he spends the night out here,"
   c. "I hope we find Boots. "He'll be a hungry and tired cat if he spends the night out here,"
   d. "I hope we find Boots. He'll be a hungry and tired cat if he spends the night out here,"
   e. "I hope we find Boots" "He'll be a hungry and tired cat if he spends the night out here,"

68. <u>Two of our dogs like to bark</u> at the vacuum cleaner.
   a. Two of our dogs like to bark
   b. Two of our dog's like to bark
   c. Two of our dogs' like to bark
   d. Two of our dogs like to "bark"
   e. Two of our dog's like to "bark"

69. Driving <u>past the park, the new swimming pool was seen</u>.
   a. past the park, the new swimming pool was seen.
   b. past the park, he is seeing the new swimming pool.
   c. past the park, the new swimming pool was shown.
   d. past the park, he saw the new swimming pool.
   e. past the park, the new swimming pool was seen by him.

70. All of the revisions need to be <u>approved by Ellen Jackson and I</u>.
   a. approved by Ellen Jackson and I.
   b. approved by Ellen Jackson and myself.
   c. approved by myself and Ellen Jackson.
   d. approved by Ellen Jackson and me.
   e. approved by I and Ellen Jackson.

71. <u>It was he who wrote the email</u>.
   a. It was he who wrote the email.
   b. It was him who wrote the email.
   c. It was himself who wrote the email.
   d. It was him who had written the email.
   e. It was he who had written the email.

Copyright © Mometrix Media. You have been licensed one copy of this document for personal use only. Any other reproduction or redistribution is strictly prohibited. All rights reserved.

72. The <u>scout leader, who had been standing in the road, were</u> hurt in the collision.
   a. scout leader. who had been standing in the road, were
   b. scout leader who had been standing in the road were
   c. scout leader who had been standing in the road were
   d. scout leader, who had been standing in the road, was
   e. scout leader who had been standing in the road was being

73. <u>Using foreign coins is not permitted in our store</u>.
   a. Using foreign coins is not permitted in our store.
   b. Using foreign coins are not permitted in our store.
   c. To be using foreign coins is not permitted in our store.
   d. To be using foreign coins are not permitted in our store.
   e. Using foreign coins, they are not permitted in our store.

74. The turtle trapped himself inside our screened-in porch.
   a. The turtle trapped himself inside our screened-in porch.
   b. The turtle had trapped himself inside our screened-in porch.
   c. The turtle trapped him- or herself inside our screened-in porch.
   d. The turtle trapped itself inside our screened-in porch.
   e. The turtle had been trapping itself inside our screened-in porch.

75. <u>"Does your salad taste okay," she asked?</u>
   a. "Does your salad taste okay," she asked?
   b. "Does your salad taste okay," She asked?
   c. "Does your salad taste okay?" she asked.
   d. "Does your salad taste okay?," she asked.
   e. "Does your salad taste okay." She asked.

76. Most students missed <u>Spanish, Math, and Science today</u>.
   a. Spanish, Math, and Science today.
   b. Spanish, math, and Science today.
   c. Spanish, Math, and science today.
   d. Spanish, math, and science today.
   e. spanish, math, and science today.

77. She passed <u>the salt and pepper, the butter, and the ketchup to</u> the other table.
   a. the salt and pepper, the butter, and the ketchup to
   b. the salt, and pepper, the butter, and the ketchup to
   c. the salt and pepper, the butter and the ketchup to
   d. the salt, and pepper, the butter, and the ketchup, to
   e. the salt and pepper, the butter, and the ketchup, to

Copyright © Mometrix Media. You have been licensed one copy of this document for personal use only.
Any other reproduction or redistribution is strictly prohibited. All rights reserved.

78. Now that both of my brothers are married, I have <u>two sister's-in-law</u>.
    a. two sister's-in-law.
    b. two sisters'-in-law.
    c. two sisters-in-laws.
    d. two sister-in-laws.
    e. two sisters-in-law.

Copyright © Mometrix Media. You have been licensed one copy of this document for personal use only. Any other reproduction or redistribution is strictly prohibited. All rights reserved.

Essay Question

Write 300-600 words on the assigned essay topic.Be sure to write in the correct section of your test booklet. Make sure you stay on topic the entire time you are writing.Write a logical and well-organized paper sing specific details to support your main ideas. Use conventional English to write your essay in a clear and precise manner.

Essay topic:
High school administrators areconsidering outlawing cell phones at school. Despite a rule restricting cell phones to students' lockers during the day, some students still find ways to carry the phones, text-message each other, or use their phones to share test information. Administrators say there is no need for cell phones at schoolbecause parents can leave phone messages for their students by calling the office, and students are allowed to use a pay phone or a phone in the office if they need to make a call.

Write an essaydiscussing your position on the issue of banning cell phones in school.

Copyright © Mometrix Media. You have been licensed one copy of this document for personal use only. Any other reproduction or redistribution is strictly prohibited. All rights reserved.

Math Test

79. What is the probability of spinning a D on the spinner below?

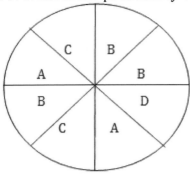

    a. 1/8
    b. 1/7
    c. 3/8
    d. 5/8
    e. 6/7

80. Which of the following are supplementary angles?
    a. 101° and 89°
    b. 75° and 75°
    c. 81° and 99°
    d. 80° and 10°
    e. 90° and 15°

81. A car costs $25,000 plus $675 for tax, title, and license fees.Ari finances the car by putting down $2,500 in cash and taking out a 3-year loan at 4% simple interest.What will his monthly payments be?
    a. $640.00
    b. $650.00
    c. $669.50
    d. $710.00
    e. $722.50

82.What is the value of x in the following equation?
    $15 - x = 78$
    a. 5.2
    b. 63
    c. - 63
    d. 93
    e. - 93

Copyright © Mometrix Media. You have been licensed one copy of this document for personal use only. Any other reproduction or redistribution is strictly prohibited. All rights reserved.

83. Find the area of the rectangle.

4'

6'

   a. 10 ft
   b. 12 ft
   c. 20 ft
   d. 24 ft
   e. 48 ft

84. A $1,000 lottery winner had 35% deducted for taxes. How much was the winning check?
   a. $300
   b. $350
   c. $650
   d. $700
   e. $965

85. What is the percent increase in cars sold in 2005 when compared to those sold in 2004?

Year	Cars Sold
2002	1430
2003	1300
2004	1580
2005	1817
2006	1900

Don's Used Cars
Total Cars Sold
   a. 15%
   b. 18%
   c. 25%
   d. 28%
   e. 32%

Copyright © Mometrix Media. You have been licensed one copy of this document for personal use only. Any other reproduction or redistribution is strictly prohibited. All rights reserved.

86. Which of the following choices expresses 11/25 as a percent?
    a. 11%
    b. 36%
    c. 40%
    d. 44%
    e. 49%

87. Angle ABC measures 150°.What is the measure of angle ABD in the figure below?

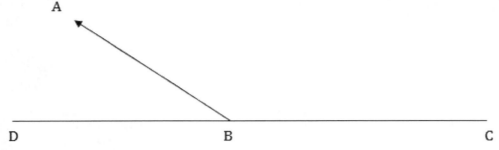

    a. 30°
    b. 50°
    c. 70°
    d. 150°
    e. It cannot be determined from the information given.

88. The scientific notation for a particular amount is 16.2 x 10-3. What is that amount in standard form?
    a. 0.0162
    b. 0.000162
    c. 4.860
    d. 16.020
    e. 0.0486

89.A woman wants to park her 15 foot long car in a garage that is 19 feet long.How far from the front of the garage will her front wheels need to be so that the car is centered on the floor of the garage?
    a. 2 feet
    b. 2 ½ feet
    c. 3 feet
    d. 3 ½ feet
    e. 4 feet

Copyright © Mometrix Media. You have been licensed one copy of this document for personal use only.
Any other reproduction or redistribution is strictly prohibited. All rights reserved.

90. A charter bus' average highway speed is 65 miles per hour while a car's averagehighway speed is 70 miles per hour.If the bus and car both depart from the same place at the same time today, how much farther ahead of the bus is the car after eight hours?
   a. 5 miles
   b. 15 miles
   c. 22 miles
   d. 35 miles
   e. 40 miles

91. A man loans his friend $10,000 at 7% simple interest.The friend repays $5,035.How much money does she still owe the man?
   a. $4,065
   b. $4,965
   c. $5,035
   d. $5,465
   e. $5,665

92. Solve for y in the following equation, if x = -1/3:
   y = x + 3
   a. y = 2 1/3
   b. y = 2 2/3
   c. y = - 2 2/3
   d. y = 3 1/3
   e. y = - 3 1/3

93. A hotel's Internet service costs guests $3.00 for the first hour of use and $0.15 for each five minutes over that.A woman uses the service for 3 hours and 10 minutes.What will her Internet charge be?
   a. $3.90
   b. $5.60
   c. $6.90
   d. $7.20
   e. $9.30

94. Arrange the following numbers in order from least to greatest:
   0.083   0.017 -0.18 0   1.03   -2.8

   a. -2.8,-0.18,0,0.017,0.083,1.03
   b. 1.03,0,0.017,0.083,-0.18,-2.8
   c. 0,-2.8,-0.18,0.083,0.017,1.03
   d. 1.03,0.017,0.083,-0.18,-2.8,0
   e. 0.017,0.083,0,1.03,-0.18,-2.8

Copyright © Mometrix Media. You have been licensed one copy of this document for personal use only. Any other reproduction or redistribution is strictly prohibited. All rights reserved.

95. Which pair of angles equals 180°?

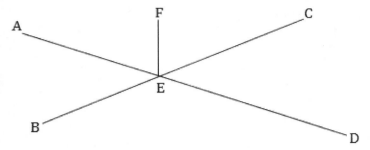

    a. <AEF and <FEC
    b. <AEB and <CED
    c. <AEC and <CED
    d. <FED and <AEC
    e. The answer cannot be determined from the information given.

96. Solve for x:
    $4x + 4 = 36$
    a. 5
    b. -8
    c. 8
    d. -11
    e. 11

97. Simplify:
    $8(x + 2) - 7 + 4(x - 7)$
    a. 5x + 23
    b. 5x - 23
    c. 12x - 19
    d. 12x + 19
    e. 12x + 37

98. 40% of 360 = ?
    a. 90
    b. 120
    c. 144
    d. 176
    e. 270

99. Write 4/5 as a percentage.
    a. 40%
    b. 45%
    c. 60%
    d. 80%
    e. 85%

Copyright © Mometrix Media. You have been licensed one copy of this document for personal use only.
Any other reproduction or redistribution is strictly prohibited. All rights reserved.

100. Solve for x:

$1/6 \div 3/8 = x$

  a. x = 1/16

  b. x = 4/9

  c. x = 2 3/8

  d. x = 1/2

  e. x = 2 1/3

101. A six-sided die is thrown one time. What is the probability of the throw yielding an odd

  number?

  a. 10%

  b. 20%

  c. 25%

  d. 30%

  e. 50%

102. Solve for x: $(2x - 3) + 2x = 9$

  a. 1

  b. -2

  c. 3

  d. -3

  e. 2

103. Express 18% as a decimal.

  a. 0.018

  b. 0.18

  c. 1.8

  d. 0.0018

  e. 0.108

104. Three rectangular gardens, each with an area of 48 square feet, are created on a tract of land. Garden A measures 6 feet by 8 feet; Garden B measures 12 feet by 4 feet; Garden C measures 16 feet by 3 feet. Which garden will require the least amount of fencing to surround it?

  a. Garden A

  b. Garden B

  c. Garden C

  d. All gardens will require the same amount of fencing

  e. It cannot be determined from the information provided

Copyright © Mometrix Media. You have been licensed one copy of this document for personal use only. Any other reproduction or redistribution is strictly prohibited. All rights reserved.

105. CF is a straight line. Angle BDF measures 45°. What is the measure of <BDC?

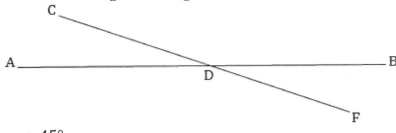

    a. 45°
    b. 135°
    c. 180°
    d. 225°
    e. 315°

106. Triangle ABC below is a scalene triangle, not drawn to scale. Which statement is true about side BC?

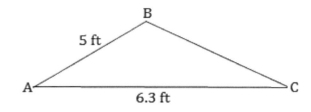

    a. It measures 5 ft.
    b. It measures 6.3 ft.
    c. It measures (5 ft. + 6.3 ft.) ÷ 2.
    d. It does not measure 5ft. or 6.3 ft.
    e. It measures either 5 ft. or 6.3 ft.

Copyright © Mometrix Media. You have been licensed one copy of this document for personal use only. Any other reproduction or redistribution is strictly prohibited. All rights reserved.

107. ABC is a right triangle, not drawn to scale. Angle A measures 30° and Angle B measures 60°. Identify the hypotenuse of the triangle.

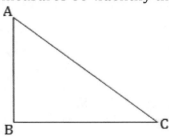

    a. Side AB
    b. Side BC
    c. Side AC
    d. Sides AB and BC
    e. Sides AB and AC

108. Jerry and his four friends step onto an elevator with a weight limit of 900 pounds. Jerry weighs 256 pounds. What would the average weight of each of his friends have to be so that the elevator's weight limit is not exceeded?
    a. 128 pounds
    b. 161 pounds
    c. 175 pounds
    d. 180 pounds
    e. 200 pounds

109. Which set of numbers shows four factors of 16?
    a. 0, 1, 2, 4
    b. 1, 2, 4, 8
    c. 16, 32, 48, 64
    d. 0, 1, 16, 32
    e. 0, 16, 32, 48

110. A television that regularly costs $400 is offered today at a price reflecting 20% off. When a customer shows a Super Saver card, another 5% is deducted at the register. What does a customer with a Super Saver card pay for the television today?
    a. $380
    b. $375
    c. $300
    d. $304
    e. $270

Copyright © Mometrix Media. You have been licensed one copy of this document for personal use only. Any other reproduction or redistribution is strictly prohibited. All rights reserved.

111. What is the simplest form of 3/8 x 3/8?
    a. 3/4
    b. 6/8
    c. 9/64
    d. 1
    e. 1 1/8

112. Most students can expect to see their grade point averages increase by 8.2% after taking Mrs. Wilson's review class.George's average prior to the class is a 72.What can he expect it to be after taking the class?
    a. 74
    b. 75
    c. 76
    d. 77
    e. 78

113.What is a true statement about the circles below?

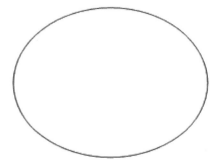 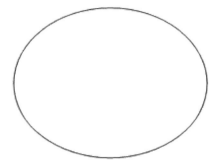

Radius = 8 inches   Radius = 12 inches

    a. They are congruent. =esit
    b. They are similar.
    c. They are neither congruent nor similar.
    d. They are both congruent and similar.
    e. They are equal.

114.Mary's basketball team is losing tonight's game 42-15.Mary scores a three-point shot.How many more three-point shots will someone on her team have to score in order to tie the game?
    a. 5
    b. 6
    c. 7
    d. 8
    e. 9

- 34 -

Copyright © Mometrix Media. You have been licensed one copy of this document for personal use only. Any other reproduction or redistribution is strictly prohibited. All rights reserved.

115. Which of the following fractions is 0.18 expressed in its lowest terms?
   a. 9/50
   b. 18/100
   c. 9/5
   d. 14/5
   e. 18/10

116. A can of soda costs 89 cents. A six-pack of the same soda costs $4.50. What is the savings per can when a person buys a six-pack instead of a single can?
   a. 5 cents
   b. 14 cents
   c. 28 cents
   d. 75 cents
   e. 84 cents

117. Which of the following is the largest number?
   a. 0.004
   b. 0.03
   c. 0.2
   d. 0.30
   e. 0.400

118. Which number is not a factor of 648?
   a. 3
   b. 2
   c. 7
   d. 9
   e. 8

Copyright © Mometrix Media. You have been licensed one copy of this document for personal use only. Any other reproduction or redistribution is strictly prohibited. All rights reserved.

Answer Key and Explanations

Reading Test

1.A: The other choices relate details aboutChapter 11 bankruptcy that are discussed within the passage.

2.A: The last sentence of the passage states that the changes are intended to restore the company to profitability.

3. E: The passage mentions that employee benefits can be affected during reorganization.

4. E: Choice A is not true since the passage mentions that people cannot be forced to testify if their testimony will be self-incriminating. Choice B is something that is discussed in the Miranda decision, which was decided in 1966 (Choice C). While the Miranda decision and the Fifth Amendment are related, they are two separate distinct things.

5. C: The choices other than C provide details about the passage but not the main purpose.

6. D: The introductory sentence should provide an overview that tie in with the supporting details that follow. Answer choice D is actually talking about the map and flows well into the sentence that follows it.

7. D: Although this passage describes an opera, the feelings experienced by the characters would not be considered "musical".

8. B: The passage uses schools segregated by neighborhood as an example of de facto segregation.

9. A: The only statement that can be validated by the passage is this one, discussed at the end of the passage.

10. C: Choice C is not mentioned in the passage. Water and air are mentioned in the third sentence. The following sentence mentions the elements and the last sentence talks about the passage of time as a way for corrosion to occur.

11. E: The passage notes that competition between markets keeps prices at a particular level.

Copyright © Mometrix Media. You have been licensed one copy of this document for personal use only. Any other reproduction or redistribution is strictly prohibited. All rights reserved.

12. B: The first sentence provides the information needed to respond to this question.

13. E: The end of the first paragraph of the passage mentions the connection that should be established between the reader and the main character. The incorrect responses are discussed within the passage.

14. B: The passage mentions that a recorder can be more unreliable than handwriting in recording notes for an interview. The other responses are discussed in the passage.

15. A: Body language must be observed to be assessed. Except for choice A, all answers must be seen and are considered to be body language.

16. A: Although all choices are good practices to ensure that a recorder will work when it is needed, choice A provides the best way to make certain that all interview notes are intact byusing two methods of note taking.

17. C: This title provides an overview of the passage. The other choices provide details about some parts of the passage.

18. D: The passage states that Florence is not the capital of Italy. The other responses provide details included within the passage.

19. E: "Burgeoned" means "multiplied," or "prospered."Choice E means the same thing. The other words have meanings that imply different actions: "dwindled," "stagnated," and "deteriorated" imply that something is decreasing rather than prospering. "Originated" means "started."

20. C: All of the answer choices discuss scaffolding but the second sentence should talk about the technique, not about the students. Choice C is the only one that specifically discusses the technique and would fit well as the second sentence in the passage.

21. D: The passage mentions the State Department's primary responsibility in sentence 3.

22. A: The meaning of "celestial entity" is described in sentences 8 and 9.

23. C: The passage mentions that Newton incorporated the ideas of both Aristotle and Galileo into his work, this would infer that he used those ideas when he came up with these laws of motion. Galileo's ideas are still relevant in the present day and have not been proven false. The passage mentions that other celestial entities have gravitational pulls. Aristotle and Galileo lived in different time periods.

Copyright © Mometrix Media. You have been licensed one copy of this document for personal use only. Any other reproduction or redistribution is strictly prohibited. All rights reserved.

24. D: The passage tells of an impending job and career situation. Of the audiences for each of the listed magazines, high school guidance counselors are most apt to be interested and take action as a result of reading the article.

25. E: The choices other than E do not directly discuss the main idea of the passage: conflict mediation.

26. E: The passage provides simple facts about cell phone text messages and does not appearto side with any particular audience.

27. C: The passage talks about teens and texting in school. Choice C provides the most accurate title for the piece.

28. B: Some women who may have run as men in the Boston Marathon prior to 1972 wouldstill be alive today. The other responses are untrue for the following reasons: (A) there is no indication that the women who ran were arrested; (C) the passage mentions that women ran as men; (D) there is nothing in the passage to indicate male bias; (E) women runners did want to race, and that is why some chose to do it deceptively.

29. A: The passage says that women did not tell their gender. This infers that they attempted to run as men.

30. B: The passage states that not all bloggers are trying to make money by blogging. Those blogs that are popular and have a consistent high number of readers can earn income for the blogger.

31. D: The passage mentions that introverts tend to be thoughtful and more comfortable by themselves than in social situations. Choice D describes the least social of the situations.

32. E: The only statement that can be backed up by the idea in the passage is choice (E). Theothers are untrue according to the information included in the paragraphs.

33. B: The introductory sentence to the passage explains that these words are used to describe personality characteristics.

34. A: Line 12 says that an extrovert's actions are "apparent."

35. C: This passage instructs teachers about how to help students differentiate between "weather" and "climate" by giving ideas on how to compare and contrast these concepts.

36. B: The passage mentions that elementary school students should be able to talk about today's weather and their area's climate. The skills referred to in the other

Copyright © Mometrix Media. You have been licensed one copy of this document for personal use only. Any other reproduction or redistribution is strictly prohibited. All rights reserved.

answer choices are based on the children's developmental level, and all elementary students may not be able to describe or talk about these, especially those in the younger grades.

37. E: The passage defines continental climate as being a climate with seasons.

38. B: The passage mentions that a mountain can buffer winds and cause the area to be warm.

39. A: The passage mentions that latitude, proximity to the equator, the ocean, the area's elevation, and mountain ranges all contribute to an area's climate. Weather balloons are used to studyweather.

40. E: The words are not similar or opposite;they are related since they are in the same basic subject area.

Copyright © Mometrix Media. You have been licensed one copy of this document for personal use only. Any other reproduction or redistribution is strictly prohibited. All rights reserved.

Writing Test

41. E: The sentence is correct as it is written.

42. E: The sentence is correct as it is written.

43. B: The past tense of "drag" is "dragged," not "drug."

44. E: The sentence is correct as it is written.

45. A: Nouns that name family members are capitalized only when used as a proper noun:
> Her grandmother ordered <u>dinner</u>.
> I asked Grandmother if she <u>had</u> ordered <u>dinner</u>.

46. B: Precede means "to come before" and is the appropriate choice in this sentence. Proceed means "<u>to</u> carry on."

47. A: Discrete means "separate" or "disconnected." Discreet means "careful to avoid mistakes" and should be used in this sentence.

48. E: The sentence is correct as it is written.

49. D: Disinterested means that a person is impartial or shows no preference. Uninterested means "bored" or "showing no interest." Uninterested is the appropriate word to use in this sentence.

50. A: Eminent means "famous." Imminent means "soon." Imminent should be used here.

51. B: Had ought is considered to be bad grammar. Ought should be used alone in this sentence.

52. B: Hanged is a word used to describe a method of execution. Hung is the past tense of hang and should be used here.

53. E: The sentence is correct as written.

54. D: Further refers to the degree or extent of something, while farther refers to physical distance.

55. B: Less is a comparative adjective used with things that cannot be counted or are talked about as a single unit, as in "less afraid" or "less gasoline." Fewer is used when

Copyright © Mometrix Media. You have been licensed one copy of this document for personal use only. Any other reproduction or redistribution is strictly prohibited. All rights reserved.

talking about people or about objects and things that are considered in units, as in "fewer students" or "fewer apples."

56. E: The sentence is correct as it is written.

57. The sentence is correct as it is written.

58. C: Sight may mean "something that is seen."Site refers to a location and is the correct word to use in this sentence.

59. B: Aid is a verb meaning "to help." Aidemeans "assistant" and is the appropriate answer choice.

60. E: Quotation marks should enclose only those words that a speaker says. Here, the speaker is not directly quoted.

61. E: Since "they" indicates more than one parent,the plural possessive form of parent should be used here.

62. D: Irregardless is not considered to be a conventional English word. Regardless is the correct word to use in this sentence.

63. E: Since the sentence begins in the past tense, the rest of the sentence must be in the past tense as well.

64. E: As presented, the original words do not form a fragment, not a complete sentence with a subject and a verb. The correct response is a sentence and demonstratesbetter usage than the answer choice before it.

65. C: This sentence is in passive voice. The subject of the sentence should be performing the action rather than having the action done to him/her/it.

66. C: The original sentence is a run-on sentence-two sentences joined together with no punctuation to separate them. A semi-colon must be added after "beautiful."

67. D: Quotation marks are closed when a speaker has finished what he or she is saying not between sentences of dialogue.

68. A: The sentence is correct as it is written.

69. D: The original sentence is in passive voice and does not provide a subject. Answer choice D provides the best sentence structure.

Copyright © Mometrix Media. You have been licensed one copy of this document for personal use only. Any other reproduction or redistribution is strictly prohibited. All rights reserved.

70. D: The objective case, Ellen Jackson and me, is used here. To test whether I or *me* is the correct form to use, remove Ellen Jackson: "All of the revisions need to be approved by *me*."

71. A: The sentence is correct as it is written.

72. D: The subject of the sentence is one person. The singular verb was must be used in order for the subject to agree with the verb.

73. A: The sentence is correct as it is written.

74. D: The gender of most animals in the wild is not known, so "it" is used.

75. C: The question is this part of the sentence: "Does your salad taste okay?" The question mark is laced at the end after "okay." A comma is not added after a question mark that is part of dialogue.

76. D: When written in a sentence, only school subjects that are proper nouns are capitalized.

77. A: The items are part of a list, with salt and pepper considered to be one unitand the other two items as separate units.

78. E: "Sisters-in-law" is the plural of sister-in-law.

Essay question

Your essay will be scored on a scale of 0 to 6, as follows:
0 –No essay has been written, or the essay does not addressthe given topic. The essay cannot be scored.

1. The essay is deeply flawed. Reasons for this score include one or more of the following:
   - The ideas are not clear.
   - The writing is not organized.
   - There is no articulate opinion or evidence regarding the topic.
   - Overall, the essay is hard to understand because it has significant problems with grammar, usage, and/or sentence structure.

2. The essay is weak. Reasons for this score include one or more of the following:
   - The opinion or evidence given is not sufficiently supported.
   - The ideas are not clear or organized.
   - Overall, the essay is difficult to understand due to severalproblems with grammar, usage, and/or sentence structure.

Copyright © Mometrix Media. You have been licensed one copy of this document for personal use only. Any other reproduction or redistribution is strictly prohibited. All rights reserved.

3. The essay is limited. Reasons for this score include one or more of the following:
- The opinion or evidence is only partly given.
- The thoughts are not clear or organized.
- The writing lacks clarity of expressionbecause of problems with grammar, usage, and/or sentence structure.

4. The essay is adequate. Reasons for this score include one or more of the following:
- The opinions and evidence presented are adequate to support the topic.
- The thoughts are moderately clear and organized with some rational ideas.
- The writing is satisfactory, demonstrating adequate grammar, usage, and sentence structure.

5. The essay is strong. Reasons for this score include one or more of the following:
- The opinions and thoughts presented effectively support the topic.
- The thoughts are clear and organized and convey rational ideas.
- The essay demonstrates an understanding ofconventional writing, including grammar, usage, and sentence structure.

6. The essay is outstanding. Reasons for this score include one or more of the following:
- The evidence and opinions expressed in the essay are astute, and the topic is well-supported.
- The thoughts are exceptionally clear, logical, and organized.
- The writer demonstrates a knowledge and command of the conventional written English language.

Copyright © Mometrix Media. You have been licensed one copy of this document for personal use only. Any other reproduction or redistribution is strictly prohibited. All rights reserved.

Math Test

79. A: Experimental probability is a ratio of how many times the spinner will land on the specific number to the total number of times the spinner is spun.In this case, there are eight possible places where the spinner may land.The D is present only in one space, so the probability of landing there is 1 to 8 or 1/8.

80. C: Supplementary angles are two angles that equal 180° when added together.

81. C: Add $25,000 and $675.00 to get $25,675.Subtract the down payment of $2,500 to get $23,175.Multiply this by 4% to find out the interest he will pay:$927.00.Add the interest to the total figure:$23,175 + $927.00 = $24,102.This is the value he will finance for 36 months.Divide by 36 to get $669.50.

82. C: $15 - x = 78$
      $15 - 78 = x$
      $-63 = x$

83. D: Area = length x width
      $A = 4 \times 6$
      $A = 24$

84. C: Multiply 1000 x 35% to get the amount deducted:$350.00.Subtract this value from the original amount:1000 − 350 = 650.

85. A: To solve, divide 1817 by 1580 to get 1.15 (15%).Test this answer by multiplying 1580 by 15% = 237.Add this product to 1580 to get 1817.

86. D: Divide 100 by 25 = 4.Multiply 4 by 11 to get 44.

87. A: Since they are on a straight line, these two angles are supplementary angles; they add up to 180°, which is the measure of a straight line.Since one angle is 150°, the second angle on this line is 30° (180°−150°=30°).

88. A: To solve, move the decimal left (since the scientific notation has a negative power) 3 places.

89. A: To solve, first figure out how much room is left when her car and the garage are taken into account:19 feet − 15 feet = 4 feet.To center the car, it would have to be parked 2 feet from the front of the garage.

90. E: Subtract 65 from 70 to find out how much faster the bus is going:70 - 65 = 5 miles per hour.If the bus is travelling five miles each hour faster than the car,

Copyright © Mometrix Media. You have been licensed one copy of this document for personal use only. Any other reproduction or redistribution is strictly prohibited. All rights reserved.

in eight hours it will be 40 miles ahead of the car (5 miles/hr x 8 hr = 40 miles).

91. E: $10,000 x 7% = $700.Add this to the original amount to find out what she owes in total:$10,700.Subtract what she has paid to find what she still owes:$10,700 – $5,035 = $5,665.

92. B: To solve, place the value of x into the equation:
y = -1/3 + 3
y = 2 2/3

93.C: To solve, first figure out how much she owes over the $3.00 base fee.For each five minutes, she pays an extra 15 cents.For each hour after the first one, she will pay 12 x 0.15 = $1.80. She has used the service for two extra hours = 3.60 plus 10 minutes = 0.30 = $3.90 in additional fees after the original $3.00 ($3.00 + $3.90 = $6.90).

94.A: Think of the numbers as they would appear on a number line to place them in the correct order, from the greatest negative number to the greatest positive number.

95.C: Since a straight line has a measure of 180°, choose two angles that, when added together, make up the entire line.

96.C: To solve, isolate the x on one side of the equation.
4x = 36 – 4
4x = 32
x = 8

97.C: To solve, first multiply through the parentheses:
8x + 16 – 7 + 4x - 28
Combine like terms:
12x – 19

98.C: Multiply 360 by 0.40 to get 144.

99.D: To solve, divide the numerator by the denominator and multiply by 100:
4/5 = 0.8 x 100 = 80%

100.B: To divide fractions, multiply the dividend (the first fraction) by the reciprocal (turn it upside down) of the divisor (the second fraction):1/6 x 8/3 = 8/18 = 4/9.

101.E: A die has a total of six sides, with a different number on each side.Three of these numbers are odd, and three are even.When throwing a die, the

Copyright © Mometrix Media. You have been licensed one copy of this document for personal use only. Any other reproduction or redistribution is strictly prohibited. All rights reserved.

probability of rolling an odd number is 3 to 6 (3/6).Reducing the fraction, yields a 1/2 chance an odd number will be rolled.

102.C: To solve:2x – 3 + 2x = 9
4x – 3 = 9
4x = 12
x = 3

103.B: To convert a percent into a decimal, move the decimal two places to the left (or divide by 100).

104.A: To solve, find the perimeter (sum of all sides) of each garden:
Garden A:6 x 8 rectangle, perimeter = 6 + 8 + 6 + 8 = 28
Garden B:12 x 4 rectangle, perimeter = 12 + 4 + 12 + 4 = 32
Garden C:16 x 3 rectangle, perimeter = 16 + 3 + 16 + 3 = 38
The smallest perimeter, Garden A, will require the least amount of fencing.

105.B: Since CF is a straight line, its measure is 180°.Since <BDF equals 45°, then <CDB equals 180° - 45° = 135°

106.D:A scalene triangle has three sides of different lengths, so side BC could not have a length of 5 feet or 6.3 feet.

107.A: In a right triangle, the side opposite the right angle is the hypotenuse.

108.B: To solve, first subtract Jerry's weight from the total permitted:900-256 = 644.Divide 644 by 4 (his four friends) to get 161, the average weight.

109.B: Factors are the numbers that when multiplied together provide the result.Zero is not a factor of any number.Answer C provides multiples of 16.

110.D: To solve, first take the 20% discount (400 x 0.20 = 80) from the original price:400 – 80 = 320.Then take the 5% discount (320 x 0.05 = 16) from the total:320 – 16 = 304.

111.C: Multiply the numerators (3 x 3) and the denominators (8 x 8).The answer is in simplest form.

112.E: Multiply George's grade (72) by 8.2% = 5.9.Add 5.9 to 72 to get 77.9 = 78.

113.B: Similar figures have the same shape but not necessarily the same size.

114.D: To solve, first add Mary's shot to the score:42-18.Subtract the figures to see how many points still need to be scored:42 – 18 = 24.Divide by three, since three points are attained with each shot:24/3 = 8.

Copyright © Mometrix Media. You have been licensed one copy of this document for personal use only. Any other reproduction or redistribution is strictly prohibited. All rights reserved.

115.A: 0.18 as a fraction is 18/100.This can be reduced, by dividing the numerator and denominator by two, to get 9/50.

116. B: To solve, divide the 6-pack price by 6 to get the single can price:$4.50/6 = 0.75.Subtract 0.75 from 0.89 to find the difference between the prices.

117.E: A is a number in the thousandths; B is a number in the hundredths; C, D, and E are in tenths.Four-tenths is the largest of these choices.

118.C: To quickly solve, notice that 648 is an even number (divisible by 2); its digits add up to 18 (divisible by 3).The remaining numbers can be divided into the figure.

Copyright © Mometrix Media. You have been licensed one copy of this document for personal use only. Any other reproduction or redistribution is strictly prohibited. All rights reserved.

Practice Tests #2

Practice Questions

Reading Practice Questions

Read the following passage to answer Questions 1-3:

Vocational counseling at the high school level can be invaluable to students, especially those students who may not know the profession they would eventually like to pursue. Good vocational counseling can be very helpful to steer students to the major or career field that works best with their strengths and interests. Not all high schools have vocational counselors on staff, so in many places a school's guidance counselor will be responsible for this job too.

A skilled vocational counselor will first assist students in assessing those areas where they hold their highest interest and abilities. A number of evaluation instruments can be used to evaluate a student's talents, abilities, and personality traits and often fields a student may not have considered previously will be discovered during this assessment.

1. Which of the following would be a good title for the passage?
   a. An Overview of Vocational Counseling
   b. Why Students Need Vocational Counseling
   c. The Duties of the Vocational Counselor
   d. The Counselor in the School
   e. The Value of the Vocational Counselor

2. According to the passage, the students who benefit most from vocational counseling tend to be:
   a. Those who use evaluation instruments.
   b. Those who are honest about their interests.
   c. Those who already know their eventual career choice.
   d. Those who have a vocational counselor in their school.
   e. Those who do not have a chosen profession.

3. The main purpose of the passage is to:
   a. Argue for vocational counseling as a career choice.
   b. Give positive and negative ideas about vocational counseling.
   c. Talk about evaluation instruments.
   d. Tell what vocational counseling can do for students.
   e. Provide reasons to have vocational counselors on-site.

Copyright © Mometrix Media. You have been licensed one copy of this document for personal use only. Any other reproduction or redistribution is strictly prohibited. All rights reserved.

Read the following passage to answer Questions 4-5:

Delaying their initial entry to school can cause some children to actually fall behind their peers in learning. Some studies have shown differing early childhood academic achievement results when comparing children from low-income families with those living in middle-income homes. Children from low-income homes tend to begin school with weaker skills than their peers from more advantaged backgrounds. Holding young children back a year before they begin their academic career is sometimes thought to help them mature before beginning school. This practice may actually backfire for some of those children from low-income households. During the additional year at home, these children are thought to be missing opportunities to be cultivating the basic skills in which they could be taking part in a learning environment – skills suggested to be absent in some low-income families.

4. According to the passage, which of the following is true?
   a. Children from low-income homes are always weaker in basic skills than children from higher-income homes.
   b. Holding children back a year from starting school is always a mistake.
   c. Children from high-income homes often begin school with stronger basic skills than children from lower-income homes.
   d. All kids benefit most from starting school on time.
   e. Learning at school is preferable to learning at home.

5. What is the main purpose of this passage?
   a. To persuade parents to have their kids begin school on time.
   b. To explain the problems teachers have with some students.
   c. To tell that all students are not starting school with the same basic skills.
   d. To explain the disparity in basic skills when kids initially enter school.
   e. To highlight the significant differences among students coming from high- and low-income households.

Read the following passage to answer Question 6:

Title IX, part of the Higher Education Act, was signed into law by Richard Nixon in 1972. Title IX prohibited colleges and universities accepting Federal funds to discriminate against students based on gender. The law affected athletics by greatly enhancing and increasing the opportunities for women in college sports.

Copyright © Mometrix Media. You have been licensed one copy of this document for personal use only. Any other reproduction or redistribution is strictly prohibited. All rights reserved.

6. Which of the following would be a supporting detail which could add depth to the passage above?
   a. The year after the legislation passed, women's participation in sports increased 45% from the year before.
   b. Richard Nixon was eventually impeached for his role in the Watergate scandal.
   c. The Summer and Winter Olympics were held later that year.
   d. Many male sports heroes became famous during that time in history.
   e. Some sports were not interesting to women.

Read the following passage to answer Question 7:

It is important for students at all grade levels to be read aloud to daily at school. Teachers should read aloud for 20 minutes to a half hour and should choose books that encourage students' appreciation of literature, increase their vocabulary, and promote reading as an enjoyable activity. As the teacher reads aloud, he or she should encourage discussion of vocabulary words, story conflict, opinions of certain characters in the story, and predictions about what may happen next in the book.

7. According to the passage, all of the following statements are true except:
   a. Older students can still benefit from being read aloud to.
   b. Student opinions are not as important as discussions about vocabulary words.
   c. Predicting what will happen in a story is an important skill for all students.
   d. Read-aloud books should contain challenging words.
   e. Teachers should ask questions as they read.

The following passage pertains to Questions 8-9:

There are several important rules regarding Five Oaks guests' vehicles. Please ensure you understand and abide by these regulations and indicate such by initializing and returning a copy of this sheet to the front office.

Parking tickets will be issued for those vehicles left in the main lot overnight. If you plan to spend the night at Five Oaks, please ensure you have registered your vehicle, secured and displayed a window label, and are parked in the side lot. We cannot be responsible for tickets issued by the city Police Department.

If you are returning to Five Oaks after 11:00 p.m., please use the four-digit pass code to enter the side parking lot. This code changes every 48 hours and should be kept confidential.

Thank you for your attention to these rules which are in effect for your safety and the safety of others at Five Oaks.

Copyright © Mometrix Media. You have been licensed one copy of this document for personal use only. Any other reproduction or redistribution is strictly prohibited. All rights reserved.

8. According to the passage, which of the following is an example of going against regulations?
    a. displaying a window label
    b. parking in the side lot
    c. using the pass code
    d. registering a vehicle
    e. overnight parking in the main lot

9. According to the passage, which of the following is not true?
    a. Five Oaks is a highly secure facility.
    b. The pass code is predictable.
    c. Police patrol the parking lot.
    d. The side lot is locked at night.
    e. In the past, some guests had cars towed.

Read the following passage to answer Question 10:
    The cloze exercise is an important component of students' reading comprehension process. When students read unfamiliar words, they often substitute what they believe to be a synonym to fill in that space in the sentence. The cloze activity asks the student to do essentially the same thing. As they complete a cloze exercise, students call on their prior knowledge and also use context clues within the sentence to fill in a blank as their comprehension of text is assessed.

10. Which of the following was not a reason for a close exercise?
    a. assess spelling
    b. assess text comprehension
    c. assess vocabulary
    d. assess use of context clues
    e. assess synonym use

Read the following passage to answer Question11:
    The Dawes Act was passed in 1887 and was designed with the goal of turning Native Americans into landowners and farmers. The federal law provided families with one of two options: 160 acres of reservation farm land or double that amount for cattle grazing. The land ownership was believed by the government to be a huge incentive for the Native Americans to take steps toward citizenship and become individuals rather than being dependent on their tribes. As the Native Americans accepted land, their hunting rights on reservation land was restricted. Since hunting and reservation life was an important component of Indian culture, these people were not altogether happy about the turn of events.

Copyright © Mometrix Media. You have been licensed one copy of this document for personal use only. Any other reproduction or redistribution is strictly prohibited. All rights reserved.

11. Which of the following facts is not a reason the government offered land to the Native Americans?
    a. to help them become landowners
    b. to help them become individuals
    c. to help them maintain their rich culture
    d. to help them become farmers
    e. to help begin the citizenship process

Questions 12 and 13 pertain to the following passage:

One component of good story writing involves showing and not telling the story. Showing means using the characters' words and actions to show what is happening in the story rather than telling information outright as though the story is being narrated by the writer:

> *It was a cold and rainy morning. The first track meet of the season was scheduled for that day.*

Instead of telling the reader this information, it's often better to have the characters show the information:

> *"It's freezing out here. Why didn't I bring my coat?" Marissa whined. "And why does it have to rain the morning of our first track meet?"*
> *"I know. I am hoping it's not cancelled. I really wanted to see how my meet times were looking. I want to move up to a varsity slot so bad." Jessica huddled close to Marissa. "Where's the bus?" she moaned, looking up the street.*

By having the two characters show the information, the reader has jumped right into the story and met two of the characters in the first few sentences.

12. According to the passage, what is the main advantage to showing, and not telling a story?
    a. establishing a strong conflict for the story
    b. establishing an interesting and realistic plot for the story
    c. adding significant details to the story
    d. adding length to the story
    e. establishing a connection between readers and characters

Copyright © Mometrix Media. You have been licensed one copy of this document for personal use only. Any other reproduction or redistribution is strictly prohibited. All rights reserved.

13. What is a true statement about showing and not telling a story?
    a. It is one component of good story writing.
    b. It gives the writer's voice to the story.
    c. It means providing factual information.
    d. It always involves narrating a story.
    e. It keeps the readers from knowing the characters.

Questions 14-17 pertain to the following passage:

It is important for teachers to model and teach good science lab safety at every opportunity. Students need to be reminded that serious accidents and injuries can occur if they are not attentive to dangers present in the lab. Review practices students will use to take great care in the lab.

Understanding the experiment is an important component of lab safety. Encourage the students to reread the experiment steps a few times and to follow all directions precisely. There should be an adequate supply of safety goggles and students should use them when they are working with any chemicals, glassware, or hot materials. Good practice often dictates having students wear goggles and a lab apron at most times they are working in the science lab.

Students should wear plastic gloves when they are working with chemicals and should be aware of methods of disposing of used gloves. Oven mitts are essential equipment when students are working with heat or flames. Remind students that glass can get hot enough to cause serious burns. Glassware is present throughout a science lab and students should be careful to report broken or chipped glass and to refrain from touching any broken glass. Students should also exercise extreme care when working with knives, scissors, and other sharp and potentially dangerous equipment in the laboratory.

Students with long hair should make sure it is tied back and loose-fitting clothing (e.g., jackets, scarves) should be removed or secured when students are working with fire. Help students appreciate the ease and speed flammable materials can become extremely dangerous.

Show students how chemicals and non-reusable lab materials should be correctly disposed of and review the importance of following these guidelines. Provide adequate time at the end of a lab session for students to wash their hands carefully and thoroughly, whether they were wearing gloves or not. Students will be using these basic lab rules throughout their years in a lab – making sure they are using good practices now can ensure their appreciation for the lab and its materials for years to come.

Copyright © Mometrix Media. You have been licensed one copy of this document for personal use only. Any other reproduction or redistribution is strictly prohibited. All rights reserved.

14. Where would this passage most likely appear?
    a. In a student's high school handbook
    b. On a lab equipment label
    c. In the page immediately before each science experiment
    d. In a teacher's science text
    e. In a student's science text

15. Which sentence would be the best addition to paragraph 3?
    a. Glass does not change appearance when it is hot.
    b. Some students may misread instructions for an experiment.
    c. Students should complete lab reports after each experiment.
    d. Teachers should be trained in CPR.
    e. Students can get hurt in a lab.

16. What is the main idea of this passage?
    a. Accidents can happen in the lab.
    b. Good lab practices are important for students to learn.
    c. Teachers are responsible for teaching about lab equipment.
    d. Labs should have safety equipment.
    e. Students can learn quite a bit in the lab.

17. According to the passage, what is a true statement about the lab?
    a. If students are wearing gloves, they may not need to wash their hands.
    b. Broken glass can only be handled by those wearing oven mitts.
    c. Loose-fitting clothing may be unsafe to wear in a lab.
    d. Plastic gloves can protect users against heat.
    e. Teachers usually do not wear lab aprons.

Use this passage to answer Questions 18-19:

Judith Sargent Murray's writings over two hundred years ago provided significant insight into perceptions about the intellectual differences between men and women. During Sargent's lifetime – the 1750s to 1820 – men were often thought of as naturally intellectually superior to women. In her writing, Sargent argued that men were not mentally advantaged, they had been educated and that was the reason for their perceived intellectual superiority. Women of those colonial times were largely unschooled.

Sargent contended that women were intellectual equals to men but that they needed the opportunity to be educated. Since they were the primary teachers for their children, Sargent asserted that when women were educated, the entire culture benefited.

Copyright © Mometrix Media. You have been licensed one copy of this document for personal use only.
Any other reproduction or redistribution is strictly prohibited. All rights reserved.

18. Based on the facts in the passage, what prediction could you make about children of educated colonial women?
    a. They were smarter than children of uneducated colonial women.
    b. They were just as smart as children of uneducated colonial women.
    c. Their intelligence depended on their father's education level.
    d. Generalizations about children cannot be made.
    e. They were intellectually equal to their mother.

19. As used in the passage (beginning of paragraph 2), what does the word *contended* most nearly mean?
    a. terminated
    b. denied
    c. concurred
    d. valued
    e. argued

Use this passage to answer Question 20:

Desalination is a process used to convert sea water to drinkable water. It is used in those areas where there is a shortage of water for drinking, cooking, washing, and bathing. Although desalination works well and is not difficult to do, it is a very expensive process.

To remove the salt from seawater, it is first heated until it evaporates. The vapor formed during the evaporation process is put into contact with very cold pipes, causing it to turn back into water. The resulting water is free from salt and drinkable.

20. Which of the following sentences would be a relevant detail to add to the first paragraph above?
    a. In those areas where it is used, desalination is a necessity.
    b. People have probably never heard of desalination.
    c. Most people would be shocked at its cost.
    d. Water is important to daily life.
    e. People should instead be conserving water.

Read the following passage to answer Question 21:

When students take part in inquiry-based learning, most models prescribe first defining the problem. Students brainstorm inquiry questions to help them learn more about how to resolve the problem. Questions can take a variety of formats and will have varying degrees of usefulness.

Closed-ended questions, those that can be answered with a *yes*, *no*, or other one-word response, tend to provide the least amount of

Copyright © Mometrix Media. You have been licensed one copy of this document for personal use only. Any other reproduction or redistribution is strictly prohibited. All rights reserved.

usable data. Open-ended questions, those that can have more than a few correct answers, yield the best information as students work to resolve their identified problem. Students will have to refer to an assortment of resources as they research possible answers to their question.

21. According to the passage, what is the best explanation for not asking close-ended questions?
    a. The teacher has to ask too many of them.
    b. They take too long to create.
    c. They only provide one-word responses.
    d. They do not define the problem.
    e. They are usually misunderstood by students.

Read this passage for answering Questions 22 and 23:

Print newspapers today are in survival mode. The past decade has been an unsettled one for national and local papers as online technology has provided enhanced opportunities for readers to get news. Add our country's current poor economy to the equation and publishers of most large national newspapers don't need to read quarterly figures. They know their circulation continues to fall.

Some newspapers have experimented with charging a fee for access to their online news. Successful subscription-based online newspapers have content that is both unique and valuable. Since many reputable websites offer their news at no charge and it is updated constantly, it is difficult for most newspapers to charge a fee and compete online. Print newspapers must figure out ways to keep their readers loyal, produce revenue, and stay viable in today's changing world. Most newspaper executives know that the window of time to adapt to the market narrows each week.

22. Based on the information given, what is the main reason for the decline of print newspapers?
    a. rising costs
    b. poor quality
    c. changing interests
    d. the Internet
    e. fall in circulation

Copyright © Mometrix Media. You have been licensed one copy of this document for personal use only. Any other reproduction or redistribution is strictly prohibited. All rights reserved.

23. What does the last sentence of the passage most nearly imply?
    a. All newspapers will fail soon.
    b. Newspapers must act quickly to save the medium.
    c. The economy is not improving.
    d. Newspapers must set up websites.
    e. There are only a few newspapers left.

This passage pertains to Question 24:

During both fission and fusion – two types of nuclear reactions - small quantities of matter are changed into large amounts of energy. Fission involves breaking down. One large nucleus is split into smaller pieces. Nuclear fission is commonly used as a form of energy.

With fusion two light nuclei fuse, or combine, to form one larger nucleus. Unlike fission, fusion has not been used as a reliable and useable alternate form of energy despite it being a powerful nuclear reaction that causes change.

24. What is true about both fission and fusion?
    a. Both involve breaking down.
    b. Both involve combining nuclei.
    c. Both commonly used as an energy source.
    d. Both are unreliable.
    e. Both are nuclear reactions.

Read to answer Question 25:

China's Yangtze River (also known as the Chang) is the longest river in Asia. The Yangtze flows from Tibet, a mountainous region in southwest China, mainly eastward through the center of China, past the city of Shanghai, and finally emptying into the Pacific Ocean. Since the river is so long — about 4,000 miles— the Yangtze is an important transportation and trade route in China.

25. According to the passage, which statement is not true?
    a. All other rivers in Asia must be less than 4,000 miles in length.
    b. Tibet is east of Shanghai.
    c. The Chang River is the longest river in China.
    d. All shipping originates in Tibet.
    e. All four statements are false.

Copyright © Mometrix Media. You have been licensed one copy of this document for personal use only. Any other reproduction or redistribution is strictly prohibited. All rights reserved.

Passage to read for Questions 26-27:

   School vouchers were initially introduced as a solution for those students who were dissatisfied with their zoned public school. Vouchers provided those students with what can best be described as a grant to attend a more highly regarded private school in their area. Some schools in our country are under-performing. Educational assessments do not meet set minimum standards, so school vouchers were seen as one solution for dissatisfied students.

   Vouchers do not always resolve the problem. Sometimes students may want to attend a private school but won't have transportation there. Other students may be content in their present underperforming school but are unsure what to do when their classmates leave. Jobs and funding may be lost if enough students leave a school, often eroding the school's performance further.

   Since they do not take government funding, many private schools do not have to attain the same standards as public schools. Some private schools may not accept students who are not of a certain academic level and academically challenged students may not be helped at all by vouchers. Private schools often do not have trained teachers and programs in place to work with those students who need remediation or particular types of individualized instruction.

26. According to the passage, what does not typically happen when many students leave a particular underperforming school?
  a. New students are admitted at the same rate.
  b. The school population decrease..
  c. Schools lose government funding.
  d. The school becomes weaker.
  e. The staff loses jobs.

27. Which student may be most helped by the voucher system?
  a. an academically challenged student
  b. a student happy in his present school
  c. a student with friends at his school
  d. a student who is dissatisfied with his school
  e. a student with a private school near his present school

Copyright © Mometrix Media. You have been licensed one copy of this document for personal use only. Any other reproduction or redistribution is strictly prohibited. All rights reserved.

Passage to answer Questions 28-29:

As a plunger is depressed, air inside the wide rubber cup is pushed out. This depression action forms a strong, airtight seal around the top of a clogged pipe and the plunger cup is held fast by the air pressure of the user. Continued plunging – pressing down on the plunger – causes an increase in pressure inside the clogged pipe and will usually force out whatever may be causing the clog.

28. What can word best describes the organization of this passage?
    a. inferring
    b. hypothesizing
    c. explaining
    d. observing
    e. modeling

29. As used in the passage, what does the word "depressed" most nearly mean?
    a. very unhappy
    b. decreased appreciably
    c. exhaled hard
    d. ignored completely
    e. pushed down

Read to answer Question 30:

Blogs can be created and written on any subject and even about nothing. Bloggers, as those who write blogs are usually referred, may write a daily dose of wisdom about baseball, childrearing, looking for a job, looking for a boyfriend, or just about what they do every day.

Many bloggers hope to interest as many readers as they are able to. Serious bloggers, those who update their online journal with regularity, usually hope to gain and hold onto a regular audience.

30. According to the passage, which of the following statements is true?
    a. Some bloggers do not update their blog regularly.
    b. All bloggers want many readers.
    c. Serious bloggers write on serious subjects.
    d. Bloggers need a defined subject to write on.
    e. Bloggers are people who read blogs.

Copyright © Mometrix Media. You have been licensed one copy of this document for personal use only. Any other reproduction or redistribution is strictly prohibited. All rights reserved.

Questions 31-34

Conflict mediation in many schools requires staff to use specific problem-solving strategies. These tactics are employed with the students involved in the conflict and a teacher or student acting as mediator. A student is a peer mediator and has been trained in conflict resolution. The student mediator uses specific prompts to encourage the involved students to brainstorm ways to resolve the problem. The students are guided to work toward a resolution they both are comfortable with. This meeting of the minds does not always successfully resolve the conflict but is usually considered a positive step to attempt to have students work out problems in a mature and socially acceptable way.

31. According to the passage, who must act as a mediator?
    a. an administrator
    b. teacher or student
    c. teacher
    d. student
    e. someone directly involved

32. What is true about conflict mediation?
    a. It always creates a successful resolution.
    b. It rarely works as it is supposed to.
    c. It involves separating problem students.
    d. It solves problems among peer mediators.
    e. It involves specific strategies.

33. As used in the passage, what does the word "prompt" most nearly mean?
    a. suggestion
    b. punctual
    c. brainstorm
    d. time saver
    e. rapid

34. What is true of the resolution within a conflict resolution session?
    a. one mediator creates the resolution
    b. it is one that will work quickly
    c. it is usually one that will separate the students
    d. it is one that both parties will agree with
    e. it is one that is guaranteed to be successful

Copyright © Mometrix Media. You have been licensed one copy of this document for personal use only. Any other reproduction or redistribution is strictly prohibited. All rights reserved.

Passage for answering Questions 35-40:

Introductions between two professional people who do not know each other involve introducing the lowest-ranked person (often the youngest) to the higher-ranking person. A new teacher aide at a school would be introduced to the principal:

Ellen, this is Jane Wilson. Jane is working in Pete Richards' classroom and comes to us from Reed Elementary.

Then introduce the two people in reverse:

Jane, Ellen Kennedy is our school's principal. She has been with East Side High for the past seven years. Ellen's office is right over there.

Sometimes a person's name is tricky. The correct pronunciation or the name to be used should be clarified as part of the introduction:

Karen, I'd like you to meet Angelique DeMarco. Angie will be working as a student teacher for the next three months in Chris Maxwell's first grade classroom.

George, this is Illiyo Lee. Illiyo goes by the name Ellie. She is visiting our school this week from Tokyo.

In reverse:

Ellie, George Smith is our district's curriculum director. George's office is here in our school and I'm sure he will be happy to answer any questions you may have this week.

Making introductions deliberately and correctly puts everyone at ease. Sometimes the person making the introduction may feel uncomfortable in the role, but those being introduced will be grateful for the time taken to put them at ease. (business protocol)

35. A bank president is being introduced to a new hire. Who is introduced to whom?
    a. the bank president is introduced to the new hire
    b. the new hire is introduced to the bank president
    c. the older of the two is introduced to the younger of the two
    d. the younger of the two is introduced to the older of the two
    e. it does not matter

Copyright © Mometrix Media. You have been licensed one copy of this document for personal use only. Any other reproduction or redistribution is strictly prohibited. All rights reserved.

36. According to the passage, what usually occurs after one person is introduced to another?
    a. they are introduced in reverse
    b. they are asked their names
    c. they are invited to shake hands
    d. they go back to what they were doing
    e. they pronounce their names

37. According to the passage, what should be done if a person has a difficult name to pronounce?
    a. skip that part of her name
    b. make a joke about it
    c. clarify the correct way to say it
    d. ask the person to say it
    e. use an initial

38. When are formal introductions most often used?
    a. in all settings
    b. in a casual setting
    c. in a professional setting
    d. in a school setting
    e. in an uncomfortable setting

39. What is the usual goal for introducing two people?
    a. make those involved more comfortable
    b. review business protocol
    c. take time in a meeting
    d. ensure the highest ranking person knows everyone
    e. ensure the lowest ranking person knows everyone

40. A city government official and an administrative assistant will be introduced. Who does the introducing?
    a. the city government official
    b. the administrative assistant
    c. a third person
    d. both the city government official and the administrative assistant
    e. it does not matter

Copyright © Mometrix Media. You have been licensed one copy of this document for personal use only. Any other reproduction or redistribution is strictly prohibited. All rights reserved.

Writing Practice Test

Time – 60 minutes
38 Questions and Essay

Directions: Questions 41-59
 In the following section, there are underlined parts to each sentence.
 One of the underlined parts is incorrectly written. Choose the letter that
 corresponds with the <u>incorrect</u> underlined part of the sentence. If the
 entire sentence is correct, choose E for NO ERROR.

41. If you <u>put</u>your backpack by the door, you will<u>ensure</u> you <u>won't forget</u> to <u>take it</u>
     A   B   C   D
home.<u>No error</u>
   E

42. Let's write the <u>entire sign</u> in <u>capitol</u> letters so that it <u>can be seen</u> by people <u>who</u>
        A   B   C   D
are driving by. <u>No error</u>
                      E

43. The<u>student's</u><u>attitude in</u> math class probably ended up having a<u>negative</u><u>affect</u>
     A   B   C   D
on his grade . <u>No error</u>
   E

44. All of the <u>students</u><u>except</u> Marcus for the <u>free-spirited</u> boy <u>that he is</u>. <u>No error</u>
          A   B   C   D   E

45. <u>One flu patient</u> had an <u>averse reaction</u> to the drug and <u>had to be</u><u>hospitalized for</u>
      A   B   C   D
a week. <u>No error</u>
E

46. Grandfather said that when <u>he died</u> he wanted <u>his assets</u><u>divided</u><u>among</u> his
      A   B   C   D
two sons.<u>No error</u>
E

47. "<u>I</u> hope Mrs. Johnson <u>lets</u> us <u>swim</u> in her <u>pool."</u> <u>Pam</u> said. <u>No error</u>
     A   B   C   D   E

- 63 -

Copyright © Mometrix Media. You have been licensed one copy of this document for personal use only.
Any other reproduction or redistribution is strictly prohibited. All rights reserved.

48. <u>No one</u><u>was able</u> to provide a <u>credible</u> explanation for why the vase had
   A   B   C
<u>simply fallen</u>off the shelf. <u>No error</u>
   D   E

49. The <u>book's</u><u>table of contents</u> didn't provide <u>much information</u> about the subjects
      A   B   C
covered in <u>each chapter</u>. <u>No error</u>
             D   E

50. <u>With Wilson injured and Anderson sick,</u> it is <u>highly unlikely</u> that any
              A   B
<u>school records</u>will be broken in <u>todays track meet</u>. <u>No error</u>
      C   D   E

51. <u>My Mother</u> still likes to talk about <u>the hard time</u> she had with my twin brother
   A   B
<u>and me</u> when we were in <u>junior high school</u>. <u>No error</u>
    C   D   E

52. <u>This class</u> of <u>biology students</u> is <u>superior than</u> the one she <u>taught last semester</u>.
    A   B   C   D
<u>No error</u>
E

53. <u>Since</u> the baby <u>was born</u> with a <u>congenital</u>heart defect, she immediately
    A   B   C
<u>had to have</u>surgery. <u>No error</u>
   D   E

54. <u>His uncle,</u> who is a <u>doctor will</u> be joining <u>us</u> on the <u>camping trip</u>. <u>No error</u>
    A   B   C   D   E

55. <u>The</u> people<u>, who sat in the last row,</u><u>paid</u> half-price for <u>their seats</u>. <u>No error</u>
    A   B   C   D   E

56. The dog <u>ran away</u><u>just as</u> he had to go to <u>work this</u> was no <u>laughing matter</u>.
              A   B   C   D
<u>No error</u>
    E

57. <u>I am</u><u>going to go</u> to the museum this afternoon even if <u>their not</u><u>interested in</u>
   A   B   C   D
accompanying me. <u>No error</u>
                    E

Copyright © Mometrix Media. You have been licensed one copy of this document for personal use only.
Any other reproduction or redistribution is strictly prohibited. All rights reserved.

58. 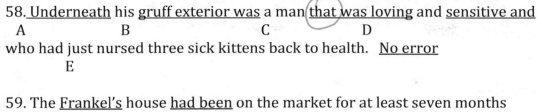Underneath his gruff exterior was a man that was loving and sensitive and
   A   B   C   D
who had just nursed three sick kittens back to health.   No error
      E

59. The Frankel's house had been on the market for at least seven months
   A   B
so we weresurprised when it was finally sold.   No error
C   D   E

Directions: Questions 20-38

The upcoming sentences are given to measure your ability to correctly and efficiently convey meaning. When you are choosing your answer, remember that the sentences should utilize conventional written English, including grammar, word selection, conventional sentence structure, and punctuation.

There will be either a section or a complete sentence underlined. Beneath the sentence there are different choices. The first choice (A) will be the same as the underlined section. The remaining choices give different substitutions that could replace the underlined section.

Choose the letter that corresponds with the choice that best conveys the meaning of the original sentence. If the original wording is the best, select answer choice A. If not, choose one of the other choices. The correct answer is the one that keeps the original meaning and makes the sentence the most effective. Make sure your choice makes the sentence understandable without being cumbersome or unclear.

60. When questioned, most students said the Math test was too difficult.
   a. said the Math test
   b. say the Math test
   c. said the math test
   d. say the math test
   e. said that the Math test

61. An only child Jane enjoyed the company of her parents.
   a. An only child Jane
   b. An only child Jane,
   c. An "only" child, Jane
   d. An only child, Jane
   e. An "only" child Jane

Copyright © Mometrix Media. You have been licensed one copy of this document for personal use only. Any other reproduction or redistribution is strictly prohibited. All rights reserved.

62. Many people were not able to figure out <u>where the meeting was at.</u>
    a. where the meeting was at
    b. where the meeting was
    c. where, the meeting was at
    d. where at the meeting was
    e. at where was the meeting

63. <u>Each student should bring their backpacks</u> to the assembly.
    a. Each student should bring their backpacks
    b. Each student should bring backpacks
    c. Each student should bring they're backpacks
    d. Each student should bring his backpack
    e. Each student should bring his or her backpack

64. If you are not able to take part in class today, <u>please set down at the side table.</u>
    a. please set down at the side table.
    b. please set at the side table
    c. please sit at the side table
    d. please, set down at the side table
    e. please, sit at the side table.

65. Most of the tickets were sold <u>the first day they were available.</u>
    a. the first day they were available.
    b. the first day the tickets were available.
    c. the first day they are available.
    d. the first day the tickets are available.
    e. the first day they were "available."

66. <u>A new state high jump record was set by Oscar Smith.</u>
    a. A new state high jump record was set by Oscar Smith.
    b. A new state high jump record is set by Oscar Smith.
    c. A new state high jump record was being set by Oscar Smith.
    d. Oscar Smith set a new state high jump record.
    e. Oscar Smith sets a new state high jump record.

67. <u>Whispering so low that no one could hear her.</u>
    a. Whispering so low that no one could hear her.
    b. Whispering so low no one could hear her.
    c. Whispering low so no one could hear her.
    d. She is whispering so low no one can hear her.
    e. She is whispering so low that no one is hearing her.

Copyright © Mometrix Media. You have been licensed one copy of this document for personal use only. Any other reproduction or redistribution is strictly prohibited. All rights reserved.

68. <u>Terry grabs the phone and talked to the police officer.</u>
   a. Terry grabs the phone and talked to the police officer.
   b. Terry grabbed the phone and talks to the police officer.
   c. Terry grabs the phone and is talking to the police officer.
   d. Terry grabbed the phone and is talking to the police officer.
   e. Terry grabs the phone and talks to the police officer.

69. She didn't realize it would <u>take so much time to clean the house she was late</u> for the party.
   a. take so much time to clean the house she was late
   b. take so much time to clean the house, she was late
   c. take so much time to clean the house; she was late
   d. take so much time to clean the house - she was late
   e. take so much time to clean the house and therefore she was late

70. <u>"This box can't be used." "The gift is too big,"</u> Sharon said.
   a. "This box can't be used." "The gift is too big,"
   b. "This box can't be used. "The gift is too big,"
   c. "This box can't be used." The gift is too big,"
   d. "This box can't be used "The gift is too big,"
   e. "This box can't be used. The gift is too big."

71. We were surprised that <u>most people's views involved</u> spending money from the treasury.
   a. most people's views involved
   b. most peoples views involved
   c. most peoples' views involved
   d. most peoples' view's involved
   e. most people's views' involved

72. No one in the room seemed <u>to notice Jack and I walk in late.</u>
   a. to notice Jack and I walk in late.
   b. to notice I and Jack I walk in late.
   c. to notice me and Jack walk in late.
   d. to notice Jack and me walk in late.
   e. to notice Jack and myself walk in late.

73. <u>Each of the diamonds are worth over</u> ten thousand dollars.
   a. Each of the diamonds are worth over
   b. Each of the diamonds is worth over
   c. Each of the diamonds are valued at over
   d. Each of the diamonds goes for over
   e. All of the diamonds is worth over.

Copyright © Mometrix Media. You have been licensed one copy of this document for personal use only. Any other reproduction or redistribution is strictly prohibited. All rights reserved.

74. <u>She sang beautiful</u> despite her sadness.
    a. She sang beautiful
    b. She sings beautiful
    c. She sings beautifully
    d. She sang beautifully
    e. She sung beautiful

75. <u>One of our bicycles are</u> missing.
    a. One of our bicycles are
    b. One of our bicycles is
    c. One of our bicycles, are
    d. One, of our bicycles, are
    e. One, of our bicycles, is

76. <u>"Are you Don Adams," he asked?</u>
    a. "Are you Don Adams," he asked?
    b. "Are you Don Adams?" He asked.
    c. "Are you Don Adams?," he asked.
    d. "Are you Don Adams," He asked?
    e. "Are you Don Adams?" he asked.

77. We have enough students for another <u>Science, English, and Health class.</u>
    a. Science, English, and Health class.
    b. Science, English, and health class.
    c. science, English, and Health class.
    d. science, english, and health class.
    e. science, English, and health class.

78. <u>We had spaghetti and meatballs, garlic bread, and salad.</u>
    a. We had spaghetti and meatballs, garlic bread, and salad.
    b. We had spaghetti, and meatballs, garlic bread, and salad.
    c. We had, spaghetti and meatballs, garlic bread and salad.
    d. We had, spaghetti, and meatballs, garlic bread, and salad.
    e. We had spaghetti and meatballs; garlic bread, and salad.

Copyright © Mometrix Media. You have been licensed one copy of this document for personal use only. Any other reproduction or redistribution is strictly prohibited. All rights reserved.

Essay Question

Directions:
Write 300-600 words on the assigned essay topic. Be sure to write in the correct section of your test booklet. Make sure you stay on topic the entire time you are writing. Write a logical and well-organized paper. Use details to support your main ideas. Write in a clear and precise manner. Use conventional English to write your paper.

Essay topic:
Cyber-bullying, intimidating a child using online technology, has become a problem for a small number of children at a middle school in town. Parents of the harassed children have been calling the school and asking administration to help them handle the problem Administrators allege that since the problem is not happening during school hours, it is not something they can get involved with. Even though the perpetrator's identity is not known, one of the affected students is refusing to go to school, citing fear of physical harm.

Write an essay. Discuss your position on the school's role in the cyber-bullying issue.

Copyright © Mometrix Media. You have been licensed one copy of this document for personal use only. Any other reproduction or redistribution is strictly prohibited. All rights reserved.

Math Test

Time – 60 minutes
40 Questions

79. What is the probability of spinning a 2 on the first try on the spinner below?
    a. 1/2
    b. 1/3
    c. 1/4
    d. 2/3
    e. 2/4

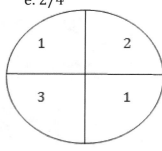

80. Which angle measure forms a complementary angle when combined with an angle measure of 48°?
    a. 42°
    b. 48°
    c. 52°
    d. 90°
    e. 132°

81. Molly borrows $12,000 from a friend. She agrees to make monthly payments to repay the loan in two years along with an additional 10% for interest. What are her monthly payments?
    a. $465
    b. $550
    c. $650
    d. $700
    e. $1010

82. Calculate the value of x in the following equation: $13 + x = 130$.
    a. 10
    b. 117
    c. 143
    d. -143
    e. 13/130

Copyright © Mometrix Media. You have been licensed one copy of this document for personal use only. Any other reproduction or redistribution is strictly prohibited. All rights reserved.

83. Find the area of the rectangle.

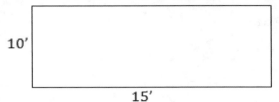

10'

15'

 a. 50 ft²
 b. 75 ft²
 c. 100 ft²
 d. 125 ft²
 e. 150 ft²

84. 30% of a woman's paycheck goes to health insurance, 15% goes to savings, and 32% goes to taxes. After these deductions, what percentage of the check is remaining?
 a. 19%
 b. 23%
 c. 38%
 d. 77%
 e. It cannot be determined from the information given.

85. Dale made service calls at a rate of $45/hour last year. He is raising his rates 7% this year. What would a $135.00 bill from the last year cost this year with the increase in rates?
 a. $138.00
 b. $138.15
 c. $142.00
 d. $144.45
 e. $150.00

86. Which of the following choices expresses 17/20 as a percent?
 a. 29%
 b. 32%
 c. 63%
 d. 80%
 e. 85%

Copyright © Mometrix Media. You have been licensed one copy of this document for personal use only. Any other reproduction or redistribution is strictly prohibited. All rights reserved.

87. Angle AEB measures 30°. Angle BEC measures 90°. What is the measure of angle CED in the figure below?

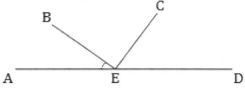

   a. 30°
   b. 45°
   c. 60°
   d. 110°
   e. 150°

88. The scientific notation for a particular amount is 6.3×10^{-6}. What is that amount in standard form?
   a. 0.0000063
   b. 6300000.0
   c. 0.0315
   d. 310.5
   e. 0.000063

89. A father measures his daughter's height regularly. She is presently 3'8" tall. If she grows 5" in the next year, how much more will she need to grow to be as tall as her 5'1" mother?
   a. 8 inches
   b. 10 inches
   c. 11 inches
   d. 12 inches
   e. 12 ½ inches

90. On Day 1, adriver averages 60 miles per hour for 15 hours of a 2,000-mile car trip. If he maintains this average speed and duration on Day 2, how far will he be from his destination at the end of the day?
   a. 200 miles
   b. 400 miles
   c. 500 miles
   d. 700 miles
   e. 900 miles

Copyright © Mometrix Media. You have been licensed one copy of this document for personal use only.
Any other reproduction or redistribution is strictly prohibited. All rights reserved.

91. A woman buys a $125,000 home by putting down 22% of the price and financing the rest. How much of the price has she financed?
- a. $22,000
- b. $27,500
- c. $47,500
- d. $78,000
- e. $97,500

92. Solve for y in the following equation if $x = -1/2$
$$y = x + 4$$
- a. $y = 2$
- b. $y = 3\ 1/2$
- c. $y = -3\ 1/2$
- d. $y = 4\ 1/2$
- e. $y = -4\ 1/2$

93. It costs Jack $7/month for 50 incoming or outgoing text messages and $0.15 for each text message over that. Jack sent 35 text messages this month and received 48. What will his bill be for this month?
- a. $4.20
- b. $4.95
- c. $11.95
- d. $12.45
- e. $14.20

94. Put the following decimal numbers in order from least to greatest:
-1.32, 0.014, 0.31, 0.308, -0.42, 0

- a. -0.42, -1.32, 0.31, 0.308, 0, 0.014
- b. 0.014, 0, 0.308, 0.31, -1.32, -0.42
- c. -1.32, -0.42, 0, 0.014, 0.308, 0.31
- d. 0.014, 0.308, 0.31, 0, -0.42, -1.32
- e. 0, -1.32, -0.42, 0.31, 0.308, 0.014

Copyright © Mometrix Media. You have been licensed one copy of this document for personal use only. Any other reproduction or redistribution is strictly prohibited. All rights reserved.

95. Which pair of angles is equal to 180°?

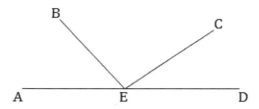

    a. <AEB and <BEC
    b. <CED and <BEC
    c. <AEB and <CED
    d. <AEC and <BED
    e. <AEB and <BED

96. What is the value of y in the following equation?
    $4y + 16 = 60$
    a. 4
    b. 11
    c. 12
    d. 15
    e. 19

97. Simplify: $3(x - 12) - 11 - 3(x - 4)$.
    a. $6x - 35$
    b. $6x + 35$
    c. $6x + 37$
    d. 13
    e. -35

98. What is 25% of 160?
    a. 32
    b. 40
    c. 44
    d. 60
    e. 64

99. Write 42/7 as a percentage.
    a. 6%
    b. 600%
    c. 60%
    d. 0.6%
    e. 0.06%

Copyright © Mometrix Media. You have been licensed one copy of this document for personal use only. Any other reproduction or redistribution is strictly prohibited. All rights reserved.

100. Solve for x: (2/5)/(2/3) = x
    a. x = 1/4
    b. x = 4/15
    c. x = 1 2/3
    d. x = 3/5
    e. x = 3 1/2

101. Of the twenty students in the classroom, half are boys and half are girls. If all students handed in their homework, what is the probability that the top homework sheet belongs to a girl?
    a. 20%
    b. 25%
    c. 30%
    d. 40%
    e. 50%

102. Solve for x: (2x – 6)+ 4x = 24
    a. 0
    b. -3
    c. 5
    d. -5
    e. 3

103. What is 22% as a decimal?
    a. 0.22
    b. 0.022
    c. 2.2
    d. 0.0022
    e. 0.202

104. Three rectangular gardens, each with an area of 36 square feet, are created on a tract of land. Garden A measures 4 feet by 9 feet; Garden B measures 12 feet by 3 feet; Garden C measures 18 feet by 2 feet. Which garden will require the most fencing to surround it?
    a. Garden A
    b. Garden B
    c. Garden C
    d. All gardens will require the same amount of fencing
    e. It cannot be determined from the information provided.

Copyright © Mometrix Media. You have been licensed one copy of this document for personal use only. Any other reproduction or redistribution is strictly prohibited. All rights reserved.

105. AB is a straight line. Angle ADC is 45°. What is the measure of <BDC?

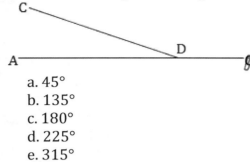

    a. 45°
    b. 135°
    c. 180°
    d. 225°
    e. 315°

106. Triangle ABC below is an equilateral triangle, not drawn to scale. Which statement is true about side BC?

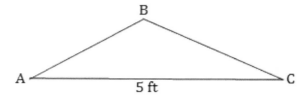

    a. It measures less than 5 ft.
    b. It measures greater than 5 ft.
    c. It measures 2.5 ft.
    d. It measures 5 ft.
    e. It measures 10 ft.

107. Triangle DEF is a right triangle. Side DE measures 6 feet and side EF measures 8 feet. Which of the following could be the measure of side DF?
    a. 11 feet
    b. 8 feet
    c. 9 feet
    d. 10 feet
    e. $\sqrt{14}$ feet

108. Mike is at a Pay-By-The-Ounce salad bar. He places a quarter pound of blueberries, a half pound of strawberries, a half pound of yogurt, and a quarter pound of walnuts into his bowl. A sign says that the salad bar costs fifteen cents an ounce. How much will Mike's salad cost?
    a. $1.80
    b. $2.75
    c. $3.00
    d. $3.60
    e. $4.10

Copyright © Mometrix Media. You have been licensed one copy of this document for personal use only. Any other reproduction or redistribution is strictly prohibited. All rights reserved.

109. Which shows four factors of 12?
    a. 0, 1, 2, 4
    b. 1, 2, 3, 4
    c. 12, 24, 36, 48
    d. 0.1, 12, 24
    e. 0, 12, 24, 36

110. A pair of $500 earrings is offered today at a 25% discount. If it is your birthday month, the store will take another 5% off of the discounted price. What does Mary pay for the earrings, since this is her birthday month?
    a. $250.50
    b. $300.00
    c. $356.25
    d. $405.75
    e. $400.00

111. What is 3/4 * 4/5, in simplest form?
    a. 3/4
    b. 3/5
    c. 12/20
    d. 15/16
    e. 13/4

112. On a typical April day at Mayes Junior High, 8% of the 452 students who attend the school will be absent. About how many students will be absent on April 20?
    a. 36
    b. 38
    c. 40
    d. 42
    e. 44

113. What is a true statement about the rectangles below?

    a. They are congruent.
    b. They are similar.
    c. They are neither congruent nor similar.
    d. They are both congruent and similar.
    e. They are equal.

Copyright © Mometrix Media. You have been licensed one copy of this document for personal use only.
Any other reproduction or redistribution is strictly prohibited. All rights reserved.

114. Tim is paid $5.00 an hour to babysit his neighbor's child. The neighbor says she will give Tim a 20% bonus for today's babysitting if he takes care of their puppy too. Tim works for four hours. How much is he paid for his work today if he takes care of the puppy along with the child?
   a. $20.00
   b. $20.40
   c. $22.00
   d. $24.00
   e. $24.50

115. Which of the following fractions is in lowest terms?
   a. 6/50
   b. 12/100
   c. 3/25
   d. 12/10
   e. 11/5

116. Brenda buys a pair of shoes for $62.00. The next day she sees that the shoes are on sale for 25% off. How much money would Brenda have saved if she had waited a day?
   a. $9.92
   b. $15.50
   c. $25.00
   d. $46.50
   e. $52.08

117. Which of the following is the largest number?
   a. 0.003
   b. 0.02
   c. 0.1
   d. 0.20
   e. 0.300

118. Which number is not a factor of 870?
   a. 2
   b. 3
   c. 5
   d. 7
   e. 10

Copyright © Mometrix Media. You have been licensed one copy of this document for personal use only. Any other reproduction or redistribution is strictly prohibited. All rights reserved.

Answer Key & Explanations

Reading Test

1. A:The other choices are about components of vocational counseling discussed within the passage.

2. E:The second half of the introductory sentence to this passage cites the main idea about those students who will benefit most from vocational counseling.

3. D: The passage describes vocational counseling.

4. C: The paragraph notes this response to be true in sentence 4. Note that using "always" makes choice A untrue. The other responses tend to be opinion and not substantiated by the passage.

5. D: The choices other than D provide details about the passage but not the main purpose – the big picture.

6. A: This choice provides supporting information that is relevant to the passage itself. The other choices provide random information about different subjects.

7. B:The answer choices can be found in the passage, except for this statement about student opinions.

8. E: The passage notes that parking tickets will be issued for those vehicles left in the main lot overnight (line 4).

9. B: The passage says that the code changes every 48 hours, implying that it is unpredictable and highly secure. The other answer choices are mentioned in the passage.

10. A: Choice A is not mentioned in the passage. The other responses are mentioned within the text as reasons to use a cloze exercise with students.

11. C: The passage mentions that the Native Americans were to become less dependent on their tribes and that they were losing their hunting and reservation life, two important parts of their culture.

12 E: The final sentence of the passage discusses how the reader is able to jump into a story where the characters show what is happening.

Copyright © Mometrix Media. You have been licensed one copy of this document for personal use only.
Any other reproduction or redistribution is strictly prohibited. All rights reserved.

13. A: The passage begins with the fact that showing and not telling is a component of good story writing. None of the other choices can be substantiated with the information provided in the passage.

14. D: The passage describes what teachers should do while working with students, therefore, instructors are the audience for this passage. It is unrealistic to think it would appear before each lab experiment, so this choice is the most logical one.

15. A: The third paragraph describes gloves and glassware. This response directly refers to hot glassware and would provide additional information to the paragraph. The other responses are more general and would be better fits at the beginning or end of the passage.

16. B: The passage provides information for teachers to think about as they work with students in the lab setting. The main idea is most nearly that good lab practices are important. The other responses seem to be details to back up this main idea.

17. C: The correct response is mentioned in line 20. The other responses cannot be verified by what is stated in the paragraph.

18. A: The passage's main idea is that one reason women should be educated was because they were the primary teachers for their children. It would follow then that educated women would be better teachers for their children than uneducated women. Children would not generally be intellectual equals to their mother, but would be educated.

19. E:."Contend" means to "argue," "assert," or "challenge."

20. A: Choice B, C, and E are the writer's opinion and not relevant here. Choice D is a fact the reader will already know. Choice E repeats a line in the paragraph.

21.: C.

22. D: The first paragraph tells how the web has provided increased opportunities for readers to get news. The other reasons are not cited in the paragraph.

23. B: The sentence discusses how the window of time to adapt to the changing market is changing. The sentence implies that those newspapers who act quickly will still survive in the changing market.

24. E: The first sentence mentions that both are nuclear reactions.

25. D: Although it is probable that quite a bit of shipping originates in Tibet, the statement that "all" shipping originates there would have to be untrue.

Copyright © Mometrix Media. You have been licensed one copy of this document for personal use only. Any other reproduction or redistribution is strictly prohibited. All rights reserved.

26. A: The passages mention the other choices as being problems that occur as a school loses students.

27. D:Students who are unhappy in their present school are generally most served by the voucher system. The presence of a private school in an area does not necessarily make a student a good candidate for a voucher since he may be going to a school he likes with friends he enjoys.

28. C: The passage explains a concept to the reader.

29.E: "Depressed" is used in the passage to describe how a plunger is pressed down to make it work.

30. A: The passage mentions that serious bloggers update their blog regularly, implying that less-serious bloggers do not do this. Bloggers are people who write blogs. Although many bloggers want as many readers as possible, "all" bloggers do not feel this way.

31. B: The passage mentions that a teacher or student may act as mediator.

32. E: The passage's introductory sentence tells the reader that specific strategies are used in conflict mediation.

33. A: The passage mentions that the mediator uses specific "prompts." The word here is being used to denote a suggestion.

34. D: Line 6 discusses the type of conflict resolution that works best and the sentences that follow say that it is not always going to be successful.

35. B: The passages indicates that the lower-ranking person to the higher-ranking person. Although the lower-ranking person is often younger, this is not always the case.

36. A: The passage says that after the lower ranking person has been introduced to the higher ranking person, the two people are introduced in reverse.

37. C:The passage notes that the correct pronunciation of a tricky name should be clarified as part of the introduction.

38. C: The passage mentions that these types of introductions are between two professional people.

39. A: The passage concludes by saying that introductions put everyone at ease.

Copyright © Mometrix Media. You have been licensed one copy of this document for personal use only. Any other reproduction or redistribution is strictly prohibited. All rights reserved.

40. C: The passage implies that there is a third person making the introductions and in the final paragraph discusses "the person making the introduction."

Copyright © Mometrix Media. You have been licensed one copy of this document for personal use only. Any other reproduction or redistribution is strictly prohibited. All rights reserved.

Writing Test

41. B: The correct word is *insure* – to make certain by stressing an action taken beforehand.

42. B: "Capitol" refers to the capitol building. The correct word here is "capital," which means an uppercase letter.

43. D: "Affect" means *to influence* whereas "effect" means *end result*.

44. B: "Except" means "instead of." Here, the word should be "accept."

45. B: To be averse to something is to be reluctant to take part in it or to loath it: She was averse to going to the beach since she was afraid of the big waves. The word here should be "adverse," which means to have a bad reaction or the opposite reaction that was expected.

46. D: With two people, "between" is used. When speaking of over two people, "among" is used.

47. D: The sentence is not complete until *said*. Instead of a period after *pool*, a comma should be used.

48. E: The sentence is correct as it is written.

49. E: The sentence is correct as it is written.

50. D: *Today's* tells when which track meet we are referring to. The noun is in the possessive form and needs to have an apostrophe –s.

51. A: "Mother" is not capitalized here since it is not being used as a proper noun: I hope my mother won't talk about it. I hope Mother won't talk about it.

52. C: "Superior" to is used here or smarter than. " Superior" is not ordinarily used with "than."

53. E: The sentence is correct as it is written.

54. B: The phrase "who is a doctor" must be included in commas. It is a nonrestrictive (unneeded) clause and it can be removed from the sentence without losing the main idea of the sentence: His uncle will be joining us on the camping trip.

55. B: There should be no commas around this restrictive phrase. The phrase is dependent on the rest of the sentence to create the sentence's meaning.

Copyright © Mometrix Media. You have been licensed one copy of this document for personal use only. Any other reproduction or redistribution is strictly prohibited. All rights reserved.

56. C: This is a run-on sentence. A period should be placed between "work," and "this."

57. C: "They're" should be used here: They are

58. C: Since a person is the subject of the sentence, "who" and not "that" should be used here.

59. A: Since the Frankels are a family, the correct usage would be plural possessive. Thus, the apostrophe should be outside the s.

60. C: Only those subjects that are proper nouns (e.g., English, Spanish) are capitalized.

61. D: A comma is used to separate the phrase at the beginning of the sentence from the rest of the sentence to prevent the sentence from being misread.

62. B: The sentence ends in a preposition, which is an example of incorrect grammar.

63. E: The subject refers to the individual (each) student. Students only have one backpack. Response D may be correct if the students are from a group of all males, but the sentence does not indicate this to be so.

64. C: The word "set" is not a synonym for "sit." "Sit" must be used here.

65. A: The sentence is correct as it is written.

66. D: The sentence should begin with Oscar Smith as the subject, putting it in active form.

67. D: This sentence is a fragment – it is not a complete sentence. It needs a subject, which "she" provides.

68. E: The sentence begins in the present tense: *grabs*. The sentence needs to continue in the present tense throughout.

69. C; This is a run-on sentence and the semi-colon is needed to break it into two simple sentences. A period would have also worked to separate the two main ideas here.

70. E: Quotation marks are not closed between sentences. They open at the beginning of the dialogue and close when the person or character is finished speaking.

Copyright © Mometrix Media. You have been licensed one copy of this document for personal use only. Any other reproduction or redistribution is strictly prohibited. All rights reserved.

71. A: The sentence is correct as it is written.

72. D: The nominative case, *Jack and me,* should be used here since they are objects of notice. To test this, take out "Jack and" and read the sentence: ..to notice *me* walk in late.

73. B: The sentence refers to the singular: *each* diamond. Each is worth over ten thousand dollars.

74. D: *Beautifully*, the adverb form of *beauty* must be used here since it is describing a verb (sang).

75. B: *Is*, the singular form of *to be* must be used here since the sentence refers to just one of the bicycles.

76. E: The first part of the sentence is the question: Are you Don Adams? This part of the sentence is enclosed by quotation marks since it is being said by "him."

77. E: Only subjects that are proper nouns are capitalized, here – just English.

78. A: The sentence is correct as it is written. Spaghetti and meatballs go together as a unit and should not be separated by a comma.

Copyright © Mometrix Media. You have been licensed one copy of this document for personal use only. Any other reproduction or redistribution is strictly prohibited. All rights reserved.

Essay Question

Your essay will be scored on a scale of 0 to 6, as follows:

0 – There is nothing written or the essay is not on the topic given. The essay cannot be scored.

1 – The essay is deeply flawed. Reasons for this score include one or more of the following:
- The ideas are not clear.
- The writing is not organized.
- There is no articulate opinion or evidence regarding the topic.
- The essay is hard to understand because overall it has significant problems with grammar, usage, and/or sentence structure.

2 – The essay is weak. Reasons for this score include one or more of the following:
- The opinion or evidence given is not sufficiently supported.
- The ideas are not clear or organized.
- The essay is hard to understand because there are a lot of problems with grammar, usage, and/or sentence structure.

3 – The essay is limited. Reasons for this score include one or more of the following:
- The opinion or evidence is only partly given.
- The thoughts are not clear or organized.
- The writing is unsatisfactory, including big problems with grammar, usage, and/or sentence structure.

4 – The essay is adequate. Reasons for this score include one or more of the following:
- The opinions or evidence are adequate to support the topic.
- The thoughts are moderately clear and organized. There are some rational ideas.
- The writing is satisfactory, including adequate grammar, usage, and sentence structure.

5 – The essay is strong. Reasons for this score include one or more of the following:
- The opinions and thoughts do a good job of supporting the evidence or opinion for the topic.
- The thoughts are clear and organized. There are rational ideas.
- There is good management with conventional writing, including grammar, usage, and sentence structure.

Copyright © Mometrix Media. You have been licensed one copy of this document for personal use only. Any other reproduction or redistribution is strictly prohibited. All rights reserved.

6 – The essay is outstanding. Reasons for this score include one or more of the following:

- The evidence and opinions are astute. The topic is well-supported.
- The thoughts are extremely clear and organized. There is logic to the way it is written.
- The writer demonstrates knowledge and command of the conventional written English language.

Copyright © Mometrix Media. You have been licensed one copy of this document for personal use only. Any other reproduction or redistribution is strictly prohibited. All rights reserved.

Math Test

79. C: There are four, equally possible places the spinner may land. The digit 2 is only present in one space, so the probability of landing there is 1 out of 4 or 1/4.

80. A: Complementary angles are two angles that equal 90° when added together and 90 – 48 = 42.

81. B: Multiply $12,000 by 10% to get $1,200. Add these figures together to find out the total amount Molly will repay = $13,200. Divide by 24 months to find out the monthly payments.

82. B: 13 + x = 130
x = 130 – 13 = 117

83. E: Area = length x width
      A = 10 x 15
      A = 150

84. B: To solve, first find what percent of the paycheck is taken out: 30% + 15% + 32% = 77%. Subtract this number from 100% to find out the amount of her paycheck that is remaining: 23%.

85. D: $135.00 x 7% = 9.45
$135.00 + $9.45 = $144.45

86. E: Divide 17 by 20 = 0.85
      Convert 0.85 into a decimal by multiplying by 100, or moving the decimal two places to the right.

87. C: Since they are on a straight line, these angles all add up to 180°, which is the measure of a straight line. The two stated angles add up to 120°, so the third angle on this line is 60°.

88. A: To solve, move the decimal left (since the scientific notation has a negative power) 6 places.

89. D: To solve, add the increase in her measurement to her present height: 3' 8" plus 5" = 4' 1". Now subtract that new height from her mother's height to find out how much more she will have to grow: 5' 1" – 4' 1" = 12"

90. A: Multiply 60 and 15 to find out how far he drove on Day 1 = 900. If he drives 900 miles on Day 2, he will have driven a total of 900 + 900 = 1800 miles. He will have 200 miles left to go on a 2000 mile trip.

Copyright © Mometrix Media. You have been licensed one copy of this document for personal use only. Any other reproduction or redistribution is strictly prohibited. All rights reserved.

91. E: To solve, first figure out how much money she put down. Multiply $125,000 by 22% to get 27,500. Subtract the down payment from the original price: 125,000 – 27,500 = 97,500.

92. B: To solve, place the value of x into the equation:
    y = -1/2 + 4
    y = 3 1/2

93. C: To solve, first figure out how many messages he had this month: 35 + 48 = 83. Subtract this from the amount he gets each month: 83 – 50 = 33. Multiply these extra messages by 15 cents: 33 x .15 = 4.95. Add the monthly fee: 4.95 + 7.00 = 11.95.

94. C: Think of the numbers as they would appear on a number line to place them in the correct order.

95. E: Choose two angles that take up the entire line, since a straight line has a measure of 180°.

96. B: To solve, isolate y on one side of the equation. 4y = 60 – 16; 4y = 44; y = 11

97. E: To solve, first multiply it out:
    3x – 36 – 11 – 3x + 12
Positive and negative 3x cancel each other out, leaving -36 – 11 + 12 = -35

98. B: To solve, multiply 160 by .25 to get 40.

99. B: To solve, divide the numerator by the denominator and multiply by 100:
    42/7 = 6, 6 times 100 = 600%

100. D: To divide fractions, multiply the divisor (the second fraction) by its reciprocal (turn it upside down): 2/5 x 3/2 = 6/10
Then, reduce or simplify the fraction: 6/10 = 3/5

101.E: Out of the twenty students in the classroom, half are girls. That means there is a 1 in 2, or 50%, chance that the homework handed in will belong to a girl.

102. C: To solve: 2x – 6 + 4x = 24
    6x – 6 = 24
    6x = 30
    x = 5

103. A: To convert a percent into a decimal, move the decimal two places to the left.

Copyright © Mometrix Media. You have been licensed one copy of this document for personal use only. Any other reproduction or redistribution is strictly prohibited. All rights reserved.

104. C: To solve, find the perimeter (the distance around the outside) of each by adding the each side of the rectangles:

  4 x 9 rectangle: 4 + 4 + 9 + 9 = 26 perimeter

  3 x 12 rectangle: 3 + 3 + 12 + 12 = 30 perimeter

  2 x 18 rectangle: 2 + 2 + 18 + 18= 40 perimeter

The largest perimeter will require the most fencing.

105. B: Since AB is a straight line, its measure is 180°. Since <ADC equals 45°, then <BDC equals 180° - 45° = 135°

106. D: An equilateral triangle means that all sides are the same length.

107. D: We know that triangle DEF is a right triangle, but we don't know whether the hypotenuse is side EF or side DF. If side EF is the hypotenuse, side DF is calculated by taking the square root of 64 – 36 = 28. Since the square root of 28 is not one of the choices, we must consider DF to be the hypotenuse. In this case, side DF is calculated by taking the square root of 36 + 64 = 100, or 10.

108. D: To solve, convert the pounds to ounces (one pound is equal to 16 oz.): a quarter pound of blueberries equals 4 oz.; a half-pound of strawberries equals 8 oz.; a half pound of yogurt equals 8 oz., a quarter pound of walnuts equals 4 oz.

4 + 8 + 8 + 4 = 24 ounces multiplied by .15 = $3.60

109. B: Factors are numbers that when multiplied together provide the result. Zero is not a factor of any number. Answer B provides 4 factors of 12.

110. C: 500 * .75 = 375. 375 * .95 = 356.25

111. B: 3/4 * 4/5 = 12/20 = 3/5

112. A: Multiply the number of students (452) by 8% (.08) = 36.16. Round to 36.

113. C: Similar figures have a proportional shape but not necessarily the same size and congruent figures are exactly the same. These two figures are neither.

114. D: To solve, first figure out how much money Tim has earned just for child care: 4 hours x $5.00/hour = $20.00.

He earns a 20% bonus: $20.00 x .20 = $4.00

$20.00 + $4.00 = $24.00

115. C: Each of the fractions can be further divided (A, B, D by 2; E is an improper fraction), so only C is in lowest terms.

116. B: 62 * .25 = 15.50

Copyright © Mometrix Media. You have been licensed one copy of this document for personal use only. Any other reproduction or redistribution is strictly prohibited. All rights reserved.

117. E: A is a number in the thousandths; B is a number in the hundredths. C, D, and E are in tenths. Three-tenths is the largest of these choices.

118. D: All numbers except for 7 can be multiplied by another number to equal 870

Copyright © Mometrix Media. You have been licensed one copy of this document for personal use only. Any other reproduction or redistribution is strictly prohibited. All rights reserved.